W9-BZX-837

REVELATION

Vision of a Just World

Proclamation Commentaries

Mark, Paul J. Achtemeier
  (Second Edition, Revised and Enlarged)

John, D. Moody Smith
  (Second Edition, Revised and Enlarged)

Paul and His Letters, Leander E. Keck
  (Second Edition, Revised and Enlarged)

The Deutero-Pauline Letters
  Gerhard Krodel, editor

The General Letters, Gerhard Krodel, editor
  (Revised and Enlarged Edition)

Revelation: Vision of a Just World
  Elisabeth Schüssler Fiorenza

PROCLAMATION COMMENTARIES

Gerhard Krodel, *Editor*

REVELATION
VISION OF A JUST WORLD

Elisabeth Schüssler Fiorenza

FORTRESS PRESS   MINNEAPOLIS

REVELATION
Vision of a Just World

Library of Congress Cataloging-in-Publication Data

Fiorenza, Elisabeth Schüssler, 1938–
    Revelation : vision of a just world / Elisabeth Schüssler Fiorenza.
       p. cm. — (Proclamation commentaries)
    Rev. ed. of: Invitation to the book of Revelation. 1981.
    Includes bibliographical references and index.
    ISBN 0-8006-2510-2 (alk. paper)
    1. Bible. N.T. Revelation—Commentaries. I. Fiorenza, Elisabeth Schüssler, 1938– Invitation to the book of Revelation. II. Bible. N.T. Revelation. English. Revised Standard. 1991. III. Title. IV. Series.
BS2825.3.F566   1991
228'.07—dc20   91-35271
                                             CIP

Manufactured in the U.S.A.   AF 1-2510

02   01   00   99   98   3   4   5   6   7   8   9   10   11   12

IN MEMORY OF

Idania Fernandez
Maura Clarke, Ita Ford, Jean Donovan
Dorothy Kazel
Elisabeth Käsemann
Celina Maricet and Elba Julia Ramos

AND ALL THOSE NAMELESS WOMEN AND MEN
OF THE AMERICAS
　　WHO IN THE PAST FIVE HUNDRED YEARS
WERE SLAIN
　　　IN THEIR STRUGGLES FOR JUSTICE

CONTENTS

PREFACE

Several years ago, the late Dr. John A. Hollar suggested that I revise my commentary on the Apocalypse, *Invitation to the Book of Revelation*. Since the book was never much advertised and the whole series in which it appeared had just gone out of print, he suggested that Fortress Press issue an updated edition in order to make it available to a wider circle of readership. After John's untimely death, Dr. Marshall Johnson expressed renewed interest in the project and urged me to take it on as my first sabbatical project. I am grateful to both of these Fortress Press editors for their collegial interest and support.

When I began this revision, I thought it would take only a few weeks to bring the text up to date. I had not sufficiently considered my own theoretical assumption that a text has a life of its own and that a different contextualization in time and rhetorical situation would radically change its makeup and content. The last ten years have renewed scholarly interest in Revelation and have generated a vibrant commentary on it. In order to do justice to the rich studies on Revelation and my own hermeneutical evolution, I had to reconceptualize the book and rewrite most of the text. As a result, a different book has emerged. I do hope that this thorough revision not only will further scholarly discussion but will especially facilitate the public's theological reading of Revelation. I am grateful to Dr. Gerhard Krodel, the editor of the Proclamation Commentaries, for accepting this book in the series and for bringing it to the attention of a wider audience.

My special thanks go to Dr. Margaret Studier, whose energetic support and hard labor were decisive in completing this project. She not only has typed and proofread several versions of this manuscript, but she has also kept office calls, correspondence, and visitors at bay. I am also grateful to my research assistants, Katherine Messina and Shelly Matthews, for proofreading the manuscript and for evening out its often awkward style and sentence structure. Last, but not least, as always, I have appreciated the endless patience and tireless support of Francis and Chris for my work. Without them nothing would get done or be fun!

The Roman Province of Asia

PART ONE

INTRODUCTION

Historical-critical commentaries, whether scholarly or popular, generally have two main parts: an introduction followed by a detailed interpretation of the text and its historical contexts. Issues of theological interpretation and proclamation are relegated to the margins. If addressed at all, theological issues appear in the form of an excursus on theological themes and motifs that either interrupt the historical commentary on the text or else they emerge in discrete references to or subtle correlations with present-day questions and situations.

The scientific form of the exegetical commentary restrains rhetorical argument and obscures the power relations that constitute it. It does so by asserting that a given interpretation of the text represents an objective scientific reading that is able to comprehend the definitive meaning intended by the author. Exegetical commentary certainly is not free from rhetorical argument, but such argument must be restricted to showing how competing interpretations have misread the text. Such a discursive suppression of present-day theological socioecclesial locations and theological interests is due largely to the prevailing assumption that the form of exegetical commentary demands scientific objectivity and disinterestedness in contrast to theological readings that are engaged and perspectival.

Just as scientific interpretations of Revelation subscribe to this prevailing "division of labor" in biblical scholarship, so also often do commentaries that have a so-called pastoral or practical hermeneutic aim. According to this division of labor, scientific exegesis has the task of elaborating what the text of Revelation *meant* whereas practical theology and proclamation must articulate what it *means* today. In the hermeneutical paradigm, the task of the exegetical commentary consists in delineating as objectively as possible what the text of Revelation meant in its original historical context. The rights of the text must be respected, and the chasm between the world of the text and that of the present-day interpreter must be maintained. Yet, by recreating and understanding the first meaning of Revelation as a deposit of the definitive meaning of the author, historical interpretation of Revelation runs the risk of "shutting up" the message of the text and turning it into an artifact of the past.

Theologians and preachers in turn must seek to liberate the text from its historical captivity and rescue the message of Revelation for today. They do so either by updating and actualizing aspects of Revelation, by translating and rendering its mythic images into contemporary frameworks of meaning, by selecting those passages of Revelation that still speak to us and illumine our own questions, by reducing its world of vision to theological or ethical principles and themes, or by correlating the text's discursive situation with present-day rhetorical contexts and problems. Those frustrated by Revelation's bizarre imagery and "bloody" content look for commentaries that enable them to squeeze Christian meaning and theological sense out of this last book of the Bible.

Insofar as the exegetical practice of commentary seeks to facilitate not only the understanding of Revelation and its historical contexts but also its multivalent meanings by interacting with the text from a particular sociotheological location, it engages not just in hermeneutical but also in rhetorical practice. By introducing this distinction between hermeneutic and rhetoric, I refer to the revival of ancient rhetoric in biblical studies that has taken place in the past fifteen years or so. Rhetorical analysis asserts that in the act of interpretation one does not just understand and comprehend texts and symbols (hermeneutics), but one also produces new meanings by interacting with them.

Since the sociohistorical location of ancient rhetoric is the public of the Greek city-state (*polis*), the rhetorical understanding of text and interpretation situates biblical scholarship in such a way that its public character and political responsibility become an integral part of our literary readings and historical reconstructions of the biblical world. Biblical scholarship as a rhetorical or communicative practice seeks to display how biblical texts and their contemporary interpretations are political and religious discursive practices. Authorial aims, point of view, narrative strategies, persuasive means, and closure, as well as audience perceptions and constructions, are rhetorical practices that have determined not only the production of Revelation but also its subsequent interpretations.

This understanding of rhetoric as a communicative practice that involves interests, values, and visions must carefully be distinguished from the popular use of the expression. Popular parlance often labels those statements as "rhetoric" or "rhetorical" that it believes to be "mere" talk, stylistic figure, or deceptive propaganda—as a clever form of speech that is not true and honest but, rather, lacks any substance. Rhetoric is often misunderstood as mere rhetoric, stylistic ornament, technical device, or linguistic manipulation, as discourse utilizing irrational, emotional devices that are contrary to critical thinking and reasoning. When I use the terms *rhetoric* or *rhetorical* to characterize the composition and theology of Revelation, I do not use them in this colloquial sense. Rather, I seek to utilize rhetorical analysis not just as one more way of literary or structural analysis but as a means to analyze how biblical texts and interpretations participate in creating or sustaining oppressive or liberating theo-ethical values and sociopolitical practices.

In distinction from formalist or structuralist literary criticism, a critical rhetoric insists that context is as important as text. What we see depends on where we stand. One's social location or rhetorical context is decisive for how one sees the world, constructs reality, or interprets biblical texts. Biblical scholarship that continues to subscribe to a value-neutral epistemology covertly advocates an apolitical reading of canonical texts and does not take responsibility for its political assumptions and interests. Once biblical scholarship begins to acknowledge its own social locations and interests, whether of race, gender, nation, or class, then scholars become accountable to their wider audience for favoring one particular interpretation over other possible readings.

A critical understanding of biblical interpretation as rhetorical, discursive practice seeks to replace an objectivist and depoliticized practice of interpretation with a practice of rhetorical inquiry that engages in the formation of a critical historical and religious consciousness. The reconceptualization of biblical studies in rhetorical rather than just hermeneutical terms provides a research framework not only for integrating historical, archeological, sociological, literary, and theological approaches as perspectival readings of Revelation but also for raising sociopolitical and theo-ethical questions as constitutive questions for the interpretive process. Rhetorical interpretation does not assume that the text of Revelation is a window to historical reality. It does not understand Revelation as a historical source providing data and evidence but sees it as a perspectival discourse constructing its own worlds and symbolic universes.

Competing interpretations of Revelation are not simply either right or wrong, but they constitute different ways of reading and constructing sociohistorical and theo-ethical meaning. What is appropriate in such a rhetorical paradigm of biblical scholarship is not detached value-neutrality, but an explicit articulation of one's rhetorical strategies, interested perspectives, ethical criteria, theoretical frameworks, religious presuppositions, and sociopolitical locations for critical public discussion. The rhetorical understanding of discourse as creating a world of multiform meanings and a pluralism of symbolic universes raises the question of power. Questions such as how meaning is constructed, whose interests are served, what kind of worlds are envisioned, what roles, duties, and values are advocated, which social-political practices are legitimated, or which communities of discourse are considered responsible become questions central to the interpretive task.

The distinction between hermeneutic and rhetoric thus has far-reaching consequences for the theo-ethical practice of proclamation. By proclamation I do not mean just preaching but all theo-ethical inquiry that is concerned with the uses and effects of biblical texts in contemporary society, culture, and churches. Such a broad understanding of theological biblical interpretation is necessary because biblical texts such as Revelation affect not only the perceptions, values, and imagination of Christians but also those of Western cultures and societies on the whole. For instance, when I was putting the finishing touches on this commentary, the American forces and their allies were preparing for war against Iraq. In the United States' public debate over whether to go to war or to give sanctions a chance, even liberal congressional representatives alluded to Revelation when arguing that Saddam Hussein was the embodiment of evil and that the forces of evil would be destroyed by fire from heaven. In a similar fashion the rhetoric of Iraqi leaders drew on biblical traditions when speaking of a holy war or the Satan in the White House. In such a contest of words and symbols, a critical rhetoric, rather than just an appreciative hermeneutic, is called for.

If the Bible has become a classic of Western culture because of its normativity, then the responsibility of the biblical scholar cannot be restricted to giving readers clear access to the original intentions of the biblical writers. It must also include the elucidation of the ethical consequences and political functions of biblical texts and scholarly discourses in their historical as well as in their contemporary sociopolitical contexts. Just as literary critics have called for an interpretive evaluation of classic works of art in terms of justice, so theologians, preachers, and all readers of Revelation must learn how to examine not only the rhetorical aims of biblical texts but also the rhetorical interests emerging in the history of interpretation or in contemporary scholarship. A theo-ethical pragmatics of Revelation does not just seek to evaluate the ideas or propositions of the book but also attempts to determine whether its very language and composition promote stereotypical images and linguistic violence. What does a reading of Revelation *do* to someone who submits to its world of vision? Whereas hermeneutics seeks to explore and to appreciate the meaning of texts such as Revelation, rhetorical interpretation and its theo-ethical interrogation pay attention to what kind of effects Revelation's discourses produce and how they produce them. This requires that we revive a responsible theo-ethical and rhetorical-political criticism that recognizes not only the ideological distortions but also the sociopolitical locations of canonical writings such as Revelation and those of their scholarly interpretations.

The following analysis not only seeks to read Revelation in rhetorical terms but by doing so to reshape the form of commentary. I will approach this task first by situating my own rhetorical approach to Revelation within the context of other interpretive approaches and reading strategies (Part One). Then I will attempt a close historical-literary–critical reading of the whole book in the form of hermeneutical commentary (Part Two). Such a rhetorical practice adopts an appreciative and defensive strategy of reading in order to make "sense" out of the "first" or intended meaning of Revelation, since every textualization involves a closure of meaning. Such a hermeneutical reading of Revelation, however, is not to be understood as an objective repetition of its first meaning. Rather, it is a reasoned rhetorical production of meaning from a particular sociopolitical and theo-ethical stance and perspective. In the concluding part (Part Three), I will therefore interrogate the rhetorical situation and world of vision of Revelation as a site of competing interpretations.

A. Social Location and Strategies of Reading

Without question, for many readers Revelation is not only a marginal book but it also remains one of the most enigmatic and contested writings in the Christian Bible. Throughout the history of its interpretation different approaches to its fantastic imagery and strange theology have emerged. Scholars have developed different strategies for reading its polysemous images and tensive symbols and for comprehending its multifaceted meaning. These different strategies of interpretation have led and still lead to different judgments about the religious and theological authority of the book, and they engender different ecclesial and cultural practices.

Readers of Revelation are members of interpretive communities that share common assumptions about Revelation and employ standard strategies of interpretation. If the meanings readers find in a text depend on the interpretive strategies they employ, then it is important to locate the different reading strategies within the context of their respective communities. Whereas marginal, disenfranchised groups tend to contextualize their reading of Revelation in terms of their present situation, scholars in biblical studies have developed historical and literary strategies for recovering Revelation's meaning. Theologians and preachers of Revelation in turn rely on such historical-critical or literary-critical scholarship when they seek either to apply Revelation to or to translate the meaning of Revelation into present-day pastoral situations.

Different interpretations of Revelation not only result from chosen reading strategies and methods of analysis, but they also depend on the sociopolitical as well as the religious-theological location of Revelation's readers and that of their interpretive communities. My own reading of Revelation positions itself within the horizon both of academic biblical studies and of liberation and feminist theological discourses in order to produce a critical feminist-political interpretation and theo-ethical assessment of this fascinating book of the Bible. Locating my own reading within a religious-political tradition and community of interpretation marks my interpretation as a particular, and in the eyes of some readers perhaps marginal, discourse in relation to that of malestream theology and biblical studies in academy and church.

1. Reading Revelation in and
from the Margins

Revelation's theological and historical location is in the margins of the Christian canon and of mainline theology. Revelation—by no accident the last book of the Christian Bible—had great difficulty achieving and maintaining canonical status both in the first centuries during which the Christian Scriptures were collected and selected as well as in later centuries. Revelation has been treated with suspicion beginning with the presbyter Gaius of Rome (ca. 210 C.E.), Bishop Dionysios of Alexandria (ca. 250 C.E.), and Cyril of Jerusalem (315–386 C.E.), who forbade its public or private reading, and continuing all the way from the leaders of the European Reformation— Zwingli, Calvin, Luther—up to contemporary theologians, preachers, and writers. Religious authorities either have relegated this book to the margins as theologically inadequate or have functionally denied it canonical status.

The more marginalized groups, such as the Montanists, medieval millenarian movements, the radical wing of the Reformation, as well as modern revolutionary utopian movements, appealed to Revelation's prophetic authority all the more as mainline Christianity insisted upon its canonical marginality. Mainline churches often still relegate the last book of the Bible to oblivion or reject it outright. The Greek Orthodox lectionary omits Revelation completely, whereas Catholic and Protestant lectionaries utilize it only very selectively and occasionally. Revelation's vivid depiction of natural calamities, cruel tortures, and mass destruction shocks many liberal Christian readers. Its imaginary world of vision and symbolic narrative of cataclysm and bliss are seen as expressions of resentment and vengeance or as religious projection of salvation as "pie in the sky." Indeed, Revelation remains for many Christians not only strange and difficult but also theologically offensive—a book with "seven seals," seldom read, seen as a curiosity in the Bible, and at most quoted very selectively.

Preachers and theologians also are not at ease with the last book of the Bible since its fantastic imagery and grotesque world of vision continue to be elusive and to escape rational explanation. Christian scholarship often judges the book's theology to be more Jewish than Christian and evaluates its theological level as far below that of the Letters of Paul or the Gospel of John. Classified as belonging to Jewish apocalyptic literature and seen as only slightly Christianized, Revelation seems not only to contribute very little but also to prove very dangerous to Christian self-understanding, identity formation, and theology. Revelation's theology continues to arouse suspicion, and has spurred much debate recently, because some scholars have challenged the widely held assumption of historical-critical studies that its sociohistorical location is that of violent conflict and persecution by Rome. Whether Revelation's theological world of vision was engendered by a situation of persecution and conflict or is the outcome of psychological resentment and of wishful projection by the author remains a debated question. Some scholars have even compared Revelation's world of vision to the contorted imagination and elaborate fantasies of a schizophrenic or paranoid person offering escape from a reality perceived as unbearable.

In contrast to mainline churches and theology, "Bible-believing" Christians, who often belong to socially disadvantaged and alienated minority groups, give Revelation pride of place in preaching and life. They read Revelation as allegory and often utilize it as a prophetic oracle predicting the schedule and plan for the end-time events which can be deciphered. Other oppressed and disadvantaged Christians read Revelation contextually as political-religious typology that speaks to their own situation. Latin American or South African liberation theologies cherish Revelation's political world of vision for its prophetic indictment of exploitation and oppression as well as its sustaining vision of justice.

The social location of the interpretive community in the margins of mainline Christianity or of a democratic society has produced *three* very different strategies for reading Revelation. One holds onto biblical literalism as a religious security blanket of rock-bottom certainty for coping with the daily threats of living in an ever-changing, complex, and frightening world. The next reading strategy searches through the Bible and Revelation for a language of hope and for paradigms of liberation from a world of poverty and oppression. Whereas the first reading strategy tends to utilize the traditional method of allegory, the second works with that of typology. Both seek to contextualize their readings of Revelation with their own sociopolitical and religious situation. A third strategy of interpretation has its social location in the women's movement in society and church. It begins with the commonly accepted recognition that Revelation is an androcentric book. This strategy, however, is divided on whether a critical feminist interpretation can engage only in a deconstructive or also in a reconstructive strategy of reading.

The first strategy. The first interpretive strategy seeks to identify contemporary events and situations that are prophesied in Revelation. It adopts a "correspondence in terms" approach that seeks to establish parallels and one-to-one relationships between the text of Revelation and that of Christians in the twentieth century. Many Christians still treasure Revelation as the most important book of the Bible providing information about our present situation and fashioning predictions for what is to come in the future. Countless Christians not only view their present situation and the future through Revelation's lenses, but they also seek to attribute contemporary correspondences to Revelation. Revelation's bizarre language and grotesque world of vision allow for such allegorical interpretations, which are often very farfetched. Revelation's apocalyptic outlook and dualistic vision of wholesale destruction are easily appropriated for conservative purposes when they are turned into an "other world" and seen as a refuge for those who seek to escape from the present world and its problems.

Books that apply details of Revelation's visions to contemporary events enjoy widespread popularity. Hal Lindsey's *The Late Great Planet Earth*, for instance, sold more than seven million copies and became the most frequently bought nonfiction book in the 1970s. Among others, Lindsey's interpretations have legitimated the conservative and often reactionary politics of groups such as the Moral Majority and the New Christian Right in the 1980s. Convinced that the final battle of Armageddon and the conflagration of the world is within sight, such conservative political groups promote a strong nuclear arms race, insist that the Soviet Union (or now Saddam Hussein) is the Antichrist with whom the United States and the United Nations may not compromise, and prepare America for righteous war and victory. By inserting the doctrine of the rapture (cf. 1 Thess 4:17) into the doomsday scenario of Revelation, such political fundamentalism promises true believers that they will not have to experience the worldwide destruction of "the terminal generation" (Hal Lindsey) because they will be taken up to heaven prior to the final tribulation.

The success of John F. Walvoord's book *Armageddon, Oil and the Middle East Crisis: What the Bible Says about the Future of the Middle East and the End of Western Civilization* provides a more recent example of how a fundamentalist reading of Revelation and imperialist politics intertwine. The book first appeared in 1974, went out of print in 1984, and was reissued in December 1990. The revised edition sold more than a half-million copies in one or two months. Millions of Americans seem to believe that the 1991 war in the Persian Gulf sets the stage for the final end-time events. After the "rapture," in which every true Christian is taken out of the world, many non-Christians, particularly Jews, will come to faith in Christ. Next, out of a ten-nation alliance controlling the Middle East, a dictator will arise who will impose a seven-year peace treaty on Israel but will break it after three-and-a-half years. The great tribulation will follow for the next three-and-a-half years until Christ returns to Jerusalem to judge and to rule the nations for a thousand years.

Since biblicist literalism understands Revelation as the direct word of God, its strategy of reading Revelation seeks to assure Christian readers that they have the truth and are divinely protected in a world full of deception and dangers, especially during the "great tribulation." It understands Revelation's symbolic language as divinely coded language and claims that it has found the only way to transcribe it into referential propositional language. The author of Revelation seems to foster such an interpretive strategy when he adds explanations to his visions or encourages the audience to decipher the book. For instance, he declares that the one who has understanding can reckon the number of the beast because it is a human number. This number is 666 (Rev 13:18). Encouraged by the author, readers have sought to decode Revelation by correlating its narrative with events and experiences of their own time.

Such a reading approach has sought to identify, for example, the figure of the beast as a historical person. Throughout history Christians have maintained that the beast is a figure representing well-known leaders such as the Roman pontiff, Hitler, Stalin, or, more recently, the leaders of Islam (Khomeini) and the Arabic world (Saddam Hussein). In the 1984 presidential election campaign, President Reagan alluded to Revelation when he called the Soviet Union the "evil empire" and spoke of Armageddon. At the same time, ironically, a flyer was circulated asserting that the number of the beast, 666, was the code name for Ronald Wilson Reagan because each of the president's three names consisted of six letters.

Recently I found a flier in my mailbox that also illustrates this approach. Frequently quoting from Revelation, the flier denounces Pope John Paul II as the boss of the Reagan and Bush administrations who through the C.I.A. foster the Pope's satanic dream of a one-world Catholic government. His Cult Awareness Network and Jewish Federation harass "Christian churches in illegal and criminal Catholic courtrooms . . . causing churches to spend hundreds of thousands of dollars defending ourselves against the Pope's, the president's and the Doles' incredibly false accusations and harassments." The author, who calls himself "World Pastor," ends by inviting readers not only to thank the Lord Jesus for having saved their souls but also to distribute this flier to others and to attend the church's services.

A second way of deciphering Revelation within the first reading strategy does not correlate the contents of Revelation with leading persons but with historical or contemporary events, in order to reconstruct a historical or eschatological timetable of the end-time events. Such a reading strategy of decoding has understood Revelation as containing the prophetic forecast of events in church and world history. The so-called preterist or church-historical interpretation insists that Revelation forecasts the course of church and world history. For instance, Nicholas of Lyra (d. 1340) believed that the book contained the prediction of a continuous series of events from the apostolic age to the return of Christ. Others suggest that Revelation portrays the progress of the Christian faith, or the progress of world history, or the course of Western civilization. Others argue that the chapters of Revelation forecast only events in John's own time. Major prophecies of the book are then seen as having been fulfilled either in the fall of Jerusalem (70), in the Bar Kochba rebellion (135), or in the fall of Rome (476). Others in turn believe that chapters 4–11 describe the church's conflict with Judaism, chapters 12–19 refer to its conflict with paganism, and chapters 19–22 describe the present triumph of the church which began with Constantine. Numerous other attempts to correlate the narrative sequence of Revelation with periods in history have been constructed, promulgated, and abandoned in the course of time.

Today a more widespread reading approach assumes that Revelation foretells the coming events of the final days of the world. Whereas chapters 1–3 refer to history and the present time of the church, chapters 4–22 (the main eschatological chapters) predict the eschatological future. Premillennialists believe that Christ will return before the thousand-year reign on earth and that the present is the time just before the final cataclysm. Modern premillennialists insist, for instance, that atomic annihilation of the world through fire is predicted by John and that it cannot be avoided. Only the faithful elect will be saved.

Ancient millennialists and modern premillennialists understand Revelation as the transcript of God's end-time plan, which stretches from the present to the millennium. Revelation is a complex puzzle which we are still able to utilize for predicting the events before the end. Such a deciphering of Revelation proposes, for instance, that the countdown of the end-events began with the establishment of the State of Israel in 1948. Some see President Gorbachev as the Antichrist whom Satan has branded with a birthmark. On the basis of Rev 6:2, Gorbachev/Antichrist will first appear as a "man of peace." The ten horns of the beast represent the nations of the European Common Market who will align themselves with him. When Christ and his raptured saints appear for the slaughter of the Antichrist and his army at Armageddon, all the Jews will accept Jesus and the millennium of prosperity and peace will follow. Such a politically conservative reading is only accomplished by doctoring Revelation with the expectation of the rapture of the saints, and it allows Christians both to project the doomsday scenario of Revelation only as affecting their enemies and to feel assured that they themselves are exempt from it.

The second strategy. The very same book of Revelation has also inspired the utopian hopes of revolutionary movements and political struggles for justice, both in the past and in the present. Although liberation theological interpretations of Revelation are also situated in marginalized communities which are alienated from their society, they do not seek to redress the present experience of exploitation and suffering by projecting victory for Christians and doom for the world but, rather, by understanding the oppressive powers of the present in light of the past and the future in light of God's liberating action. Such a strategy of reading Revelation seeks to offer not only a way for understanding and naming the powers of evil but also a vision of justice and well-being that motivates the reader to engage in resistance and struggle for change.

For instance, the imagery of chapters 13 and 17–18 as well as chapters 20–21 is very popular with the peasants and poor of Central and South America who are reading the Bible in Christian base-communities. Since Revelation depicts the exploitation of the poor and the concentration of wealth in the hands of the powerful, the injustices perpetrated by the colonialist state, and a society that has grown obscene by perpetrating stark contrasts between rich and poor, they can read it as speaking to their own situation of poverty and oppression. Revelation's insistence that anyone who resists the state's and society's oppressive powers will be killed resonates with their own experience of "death-squads" and the "disappeared." Their reading of Revelation does not, however, lead to despair. Its vision of justice and of a world free of hunger and evil engenders hope and the courage to struggle.

Although liberation theological readings sometimes also adopt the *correspondence in terms* approach, they generally employ a more typological reading strategy that seeks to establish a *correspondence in relationships* between Revelation in its context and themselves in their own sociopolitical context. Such a reading strategy can utilize Revelation in its sociopolitical context as a canonical prototype and as a utopian language resource for illuminating present situations of suffering and injustice. Just as the author of Revelation has used, for example, the Exodus of Israel or the eschatological vision of Ezekiel for giving a prophetic interpretation of his own sociopolitical situation, so do liberation theologians utilize Revelation for the theological interpretation of their own historical situation.

In his *Letter from a Birmingham Jail,* Martin Luther King, Jr., echoes the language and images of Revelation when interpreting experiences and hopes in the struggle for the civil rights of African-Americans; Allan Boesak's commentary *Comfort and Protest* contextualizes Revelation in the struggle against apartheid in South Africa; and Daniel Berrigan penned his reflection on Revelation, *Nightmare of God,* while imprisoned for his activities in support of anti–nuclear-war protests. Even secular movements that seek to prevent nuclear holocaust or the ecological destruction of the earth allude to scenarios of the Apocalypse. In contrast to apocalyptic fundamentalism, which promises salvation to the righteous, such interpretations seek to motivate people to action by insisting that no one will be saved in a nuclear holocaust.

Martin Luther King's *Letter from a Birmingham Jail* is a particularly good example for such a typological interpretation of the language and vision of Revelation. King can utilize the persuasive power of Revelation's world of vision because he addresses experiences and hopes similar to those that determine the theology of Revelation. In the crude outline of this letter scribbled on toilet paper in jail, three topics emerge: the ethics of Christian commitment; the judgment of God upon the dehumanizing power of White America; and finally, allusions to the New Jerusalem, echoing King's famous "I Have a Dream" speech. Just as John's vision was nourished by prophetic and apocalyptic writings, so Martin Luther King's is modeled after the visionary rhetoric of Revelation. His experience of the oppression of his people and his own imprisonment led him to underscore the political implications of this Christian theology for the present day.

King's indictment of racist, White America would be completely misunderstood if it were construed as "hatred of civilization," or as "envy deficient of Christian love," or as psychological displacement and repression of the "will to power." To construe King's indictment as such would mean to adopt the perspective of well-to-do White Americans who do not experience the same harassment, malnutrition, drug threat, discrimination, despair, and murder that constitute the daily experience of the black underclass. If one has experienced the dehumanizing power of racism as a life-destroying, evil power, one will grasp Revelation's outcry for justice. In a context of oppression, Revelation's depiction of evil and judgment is not seen as a wishful projection of revenge and bliss that is engendered by the author's limited perception of reality. Rather, it is understood as an inspired promise of justice and liberation given to those who are now suffering from dehumanizing systems of oppression.

The third strategy. The interpretation of Revelation is much more controverted in feminist critical readings—a controversy that seems to revolve around different understandings of grammatical gender and androcentric (male-centered) symbolic language. Feminist criticism has itself developed two reading strategies based on two different understandings of the power of language: One assumes linguistic-symbolic determinism; the other understands androcentric language as a conventional tool creating and negotiating meaning in specific contexts. This different understanding of language continues the debate on whether grammatical gender is natural or whether it is a classificatory system that does not reflect any commonsense division of word meanings into masculine, feminine, and inanimate-neuter. This debate is not a new invention of feminism, but it has been carried on by grammarians and linguists since antiquity. Whereas grammarians and linguists tend to obfuscate the sociopolitical significance of this debate, feminist analysis stresses the significance of language and symbolism in women's struggle against androcentric self-alienation and patriarchal oppression. The debate around the Inclusive Language Lectionary has amply documented the import of this debate.

The first feminist strategy of reading takes the androcentric, linguistic-cultural, sex/gender system as a self-contained, closed system signifying reality. Insofar as this reading strategy accepts this self-contained and naturalized sex/gender categorization itself, its critical task consists either in tracing its inscription in the text of Revelation or in revalorizing female/feminine over and against male/masculine. Such a feminist analysis, for instance, traces and highlights the grammatically masculine language of Revelation that makes women invisible or marginal in the text and therefore maintains that the inscribed and the intended audience of Revelation is male. Such language, moreover, as when reading Rev 14:4 ("these who have not defiled themselves with women") in a literalist sense, insists that the true followers of the Lamb are male ascetic warriors.

By focusing on the androcentric linguistic medium, this first feminist reading strategy critiques Revelation's symbolic construction of evil as "gendered" and takes issue with its stark oppositional dualism. Women are symbolized in male terms either as "the whore" or as "the good woman." Both the image of "Babylon the great, mother of harlots and of earth's abominations" (Rev 17:5) and the celebration of her destruction express male desire and hatred for the whore, whereas the image of the "Bride, the Wife of the Lamb" (21:9) signifies the utopia of controlled male desires. Whereas the unconscious desires of men are redirected, female desire for power is not accepted but punished. The positive female images of Revelation, the figure of the woman clothed with the sun and that of the Bride of the Lamb, are silent, passive, powerless, sexually controlled, and pure. Reading Revelation through the eyeglasses or grid of the sex/gender system makes readers conscious of the all-pervasive androcentric ideology of Western culture within which we approach the interpretation of texts and traditions such as Revelation. It does not, however, challenge this cultural androcentric perspective of reality; but by elaborating its sex/gender inscriptions, it reinscribes this system as a self-contained totality. Such an interpretation seeks to make readers conscious of internalized male identifications, but it cannot reclaim cultural texts and traditions for women.

The second feminist strategy does not focus on the androcentric linguistic medium but on the practice of reading. It does not assume linguistic determinism but understands language as a convention or tool that enables readers to negotiate and create meanings in specific contexts and situations. It therefore consciously asserts the interpreter's agency, subjecthood, contextuality, particularity, stance, and perspective when reading Revelation. Conversely, it rejects sexist assumptions such as centricity (male as central, female as peripheral), exclusivity (male as focal point, female as marginal), isolation (male as self, female as other), and subjectification (male as agent and subject, female as passive object).

If language is not a straitjacket into which our thoughts must be forced or a naturalized closed system, but if it is a medium that is affected by social conditions and that changes in response to social changes, then writing, translation, and interpretation becomes a site of struggle for change. In contradistinction to linguistic determinism, such a rhetorical understanding of language does not identify grammatical gender with "natural" sex. It understands that grammatically masculine language can function both as gender-specific and as generic language. In their interaction with a text, readers decide how to read such language in specific linguistic and social contexts. If they borrow critical methods and theories that valorize the sex/gender system and grid of reading, they risk magnifying the androcentric marginalization, objectification alienation, and negation of women inscribed in the text. In order to break through the reading eyeglasses, grid, or register of the totalizing sex/gender system, interpreters must adopt methods and approaches that undermine the androcentric-reality construction of the text. Throughout the centuries, women have read and identified with great literature not because they were totally self-alienated, but because they read it as "common literature" with whose humanist values and visions they could identify.

In the following commentary I seek to engage such a feminist strategy of rhetorical reading in three ways: First, I translate and read the grammatically masculine language of Revelation as conventional generic language, unless its interrogation indicates that such language functions as gender-specific language in a particular context and seeks to instill patriarchal meanings. Second, I translate and read the sexual language and female images in Revelation first as "conventional" language that must be understood in its traditional and present-meaning contexts. Whoring and fornication as metaphors for idolatry, as well as the symbolic understanding of Israel as bride and wife of Yahweh, are part and parcel of the prophetic-apocalyptic tradition. They must be subjected to a feminist critique, but their gendered meaning can not be assumed as primary within the narrative contextualization of Revelation.

Finally, I do not read Revelation just in terms of the sex/gender system but with reference to the Western classical patriarchal system and its interlocking structures of racism, classism, colonialism, and sexism. Such a reading will, for instance, pay attention not only to the sexual characterization of the figure of Babylon but also to its description in terms of high status, ruling power, egregious wealth, and divine aspirations. Such a complex analysis is important for a critical feminist-liberationist interpretation of Revelation because multicultural studies have shown that so-called "first" world writers and readers place sexual-psychological problems in the foreground, whereas those from the so-called "third" world focus on sociopolitical experience. In order to engage in such a differentiated reading of Revelation's androcentric language and text in interaction with alternative interpretations, a feminist-liberationist strategy of rhetorical reading employs not only literary-cultural but also historical-theological modes of analysis.

2. *Scientific Historical-Critical and Literary-Critical Readings*

Although scientific exegesis of Revelation claims to be objective and disinterested, it is nevertheless also practiced from within a community of interpretation. Its sociopolitical location is the university with its preconceived notions of language and reality. Biblical scholars do not read Revelation as a code by which to decipher events of our own time. Rather, either they study Revelation as a historical source whose information can be objectively transcribed or they understand Revelation as dramatic visionary literature whose undecidability of meaning can never be fixed in a definite reading. Both strategies of interpretation share the social location of the Enlightenment university. They participate in an interpretive community dedicated to rational, scientific, and value-detached inquiry.

Their research ethos insists that readers of Revelation must silence their own interests and abstract from their own sociopolitical situation in order to respect the alien character and historical chasm between us and Revelation. What makes scientific biblical interpretation possible is radical detachment— emotional, intellectual, and political distanciation. Disinterested and dispassionate scholarship enables biblical critics to enter the minds and worlds of biblical texts, to step out of our own time, and to study history or literature on its own terms, unencumbered by contemporary experience, values, and interests. Apolitical detachment, objective positivism, and scientific value-neutrality are the rhetorical postures that determine the interpretive strategies of scientific biblical scholarship. This rhetoric of disinterestedness and presupposition-free exegesis silences reflection on the political interests and functions of biblical scholarship.

The scientific ethos of biblical scholarship was shaped by its struggle to free itself from dogmatic controls and ecclesiastic hegemony. It corresponds to the rise of the university and to the increased professionalization of academic life. Since the scientific ethos and freedom of objective inquiry were established in the context of several heresy trials at the turn of the twentieth century, biblical scholarship often continues to reject all overt theological and ecclesial engagement as unscientific. The positivist stance of biblical studies and its ostensibly value-free scientific modes of science deny the ideological character of its readings and mask its historical-social location and interests. By accepting the pretense of value-free positivism in scientific biblical scholarship, mainline churches also subscribe to a reading strategy that does not critically investigate but, rather, represses its sociopolitical location and function. Let us consider two aspects of such repression.

The first aspect. Since the advent of scientific historical-critical interpretation, scholars no longer search Revelation for predictions of future events or seek to decipher its schedule for the end time. Instead they study this book as a historical source-text that provides a window to its own time and community. Historical-critical interpretation utilizes the same methods—philology, source, form, redaction, cultural, and history-of-religions analysis—which have been developed for the study of the Gospels or the narrative literature of the Hebrew Bible in order to establish the historical referents of the persons and events about which the text speaks.

Insofar as historical-critical exegesis subscribes to such a referential under-standing of language as reflection of reality, it is little equipped to appreciate the polyvalent symbolic language of Revelation; but instead, it seeks to reduce it to a *true* one-to-one meaning. Since the author, for instance, declares in 13:18 that the number of the beast, 666, is a human number, much effort has been expended to identify exactly the historical person to whom the number refers. The explanation of the author alludes to the fact that the ancient Greeks and Hebrews could also use the letters of the alphabet in place of numbers. The first nine letters were given the values 1 to 9; the second nine letters were given the values 10 to 90; and the last letters were valued in the hundreds. There were no letters *j* and *w* in Greek but *xi* between *n* and *o* substitutes for *q*. In order to arrive at the number of a name, one has to add up the number of the letters. The numerical value of *Jesus* in Greek is 888. The English name *Mary Smith* would have the number 848.

Since the number 666 refers to different letters depending on whether the Greek, Hebrew, or English alphabets are utilized, it is difficult to establish an objective one-to-one meaning not only between numbers and letters but also between numbers and the historical referent. Despite centuries of puzzling over this problem, scholars have yet to agree on whether 666 refers to Nero, Caligula, Domitian, or any other historical referent. The number 666 is a polysemous symbol that defies referential analysis. Although the original readers might have known whom the author had in mind, they did so not because they could figure out the meaning of 666 but because they knew the historical referent and then deciphered the meaning of the number.

Frustrated by the ineffectiveness of historical methods to make sense out of the polyvalent symbolic narrative of Revelation, biblical scholarship has ne-glected serious study of Revelation until very recently. Whereas source-critical and history-of-religions analyses that focused on the historical sources rather than on the contextual meaning of the book proliferated at the begin-ning of this century, later scholarship has tended to relegate Revelation to the fringes of biblical studies. In the early 1960s, one of my professors argued, for example, that I should write my dissertation on Revelation because "femi-nine intuition" might be able to grasp what "masculine reason" could not "penetrate."

The historical-critical method has proved most fruitful in delineating Revelation's historical-social setting and in elaborating its context within the history of cultures and religions. Such an approach uses the text of Revelation as an admittedly very clouded window both to the actual situation of the author and his communities as well as to the historical reality of Asia Minor at the end of the first century C.E. Much of such historical interpretation depends on the fact that the majority of scholars situate the book in the cultural and religious context of Asia Minor at the end of the first century. It relies on a broad-based scholarly consensus that John wrote down "the words of prophecy" during the reign of the Roman emperor Domitian (81–96 C.E.). Some ancient traditions and some modern commentators claim that Revelation was written during the regime of Trajan (98–117 C.E.); others date it as early as the reign of Nero (54–68 C.E.). John's work seems best dated either in the time of Domitian or of Trajan, since it seems to allude to the expectation of Nero's return. Tradition also suggests dating the book in the last years of the reign of Domitian, since Irenaeus (ca. 180 C.E.), who was born in Asia Minor, already assumed this date. The place of its origin is, according to the author's own testimony, Asia Minor.

Assuming that the author aims to depict historical events of his own time, which he understands as the end time, scholars seek to establish traces of such historical events in the narrative symbolization and sequence of the book. For instance, scholars who assume that Revelation was written under Domitian agree that Babylon refers to Rome, whereas those dating the book under Nero maintain that it refers to Jerusalem. Whereas most scholars agree that chapters 1–3 reflect the situation of the church in Asia Minor, they disagree on whether the whole book refers to the church and its political situation or whether chapters 4–12 depict God's visitation and judgment on Israel and chapters 13–19 narrate God's impending judgment on Rome.

In order to illuminate the sociocultural and religiohistorical context of Revelation, scholars have focused especially on the so-called seven letters as historical sources. Such a historical-referential analysis tends to separate the letters as a reflection of historical reality from the apocalyptic visionary part of the book, which projects visions of the future in the language of traditional apocalypticism. If the so-called letters are divorced from the overall work and are understood as actual historical letters or as a report of the author describing his historical situation, then interpreters overlook the apocalyptic-literary character of the so-called letters. The so-called seven letters as well as the rest of the book are construed as an apocalyptic vision and must be read as such.

Insofar as historical-critical interpretation attempts to identify figures and situations in the narrative with certain historical persons and events, it adopts decoding strategies that understand language as reflecting reality. Such a hermeneutical understanding, however, forces preachers and theologians to reduce the book's rich world of meaning to selective propositional statements.

In seeking to articulate either a "pastoral application" for today or a deeper theological "true meaning" of the book's historically limited and particularized meaning, theological interpretation tends to fall back on an idealistic or "spiritualizing" reading that decodes Revelation's symbolic narrative as referring to universal human experience or timeless truths. Thus historical-critical exegesis is in danger of either reducing the symbolic language of the book to code or of depoliticizing the particular historical-rhetorical situation of Revelation in such a way that it refers to timeless truths, universal principles, and scientific interpretations that obfuscate its sociopolitical location and interest.

The second aspect. Throughout history Revelation not only has engendered speculation about the course of history or the timing of the end events, but it has also inspired Western cultural imagination. More than any other book of the Christian canon, Revelation has profoundly influenced Western art and literature. Although the text of Revelation defies visualization, works of art—from those of early Christian basilicas through the medieval manuscript illuminations of Queen Eleanor's Apocalypse, the Angers tapestry, and Dürer's woodcuts, and from the miniatures of the Flemish Apocalypse to Blake's etchings and Picasso's Guernica— all have drawn their inspiration from Revelation. The fact that so many great works of art have attempted to pictorialize the dazzling succession of images indicates that the mythic symbols of the book function as tensive symbols and not as literary code. Their evocative power has engendered not only visual art but also works of music, drama, and film.

Literary-critical reading of Revelation not only recognizes the polyvalent character of Revelation's language and symbols but also tends to depoliticize and universalize its own interpretation. At least since the eighteenth century, scholars have paid some attention to the literary character, symbolic language, mythic narrative, and rhetorical function of Revelation, although the main focus of Revelation scholarship remained historical until very recently. In the past ten years or so scholars have come to appreciate anew the literary power of the work. This appreciation, however, tends to exclude historical readings insofar as it objectifies and universalizes the text by abstracting it from its sociopolitical situation and interests.

Eighteenth-century interpreters had already acknowledged that apocalyptic language is akin to poetic language, and they were well aware that in antiquity prophecy was considered similar to poetry. Nevertheless, historical-critical scholarship has tended to relegate apocalyptic language to mere form from which the historical or theological content may be distilled. Interpreters tend to reduce mythological symbolization to historical facts, timeless principles, or ontological archetypes, since the book's often bizarre imagery or crude mythology offends rational-logical sensibilities. The theological evaluation of

Revelation as a myth of revenge and a drama of resentment, deemed incompatible with a Christian theology of love and forgiveness, further contributes to scholarly misapprehension.

Literary interpretations of Revelation's mythopoetic language therefore object to the understanding of Revelation as a system of signs in need of decoding, of symbols that can be equated with historical events, or of images forecasting historical incidents and events. They argue that the meaning of Revelation cannot be derived from its sources and traditions nor be found in individual text-segments. Rather, interpreters must take into account the literary conventions of the time and judge each statement or segment within the overall literary configuration of the book. In addition, it must be recognized that each act of reading is a creative performance that recreates the meaning of a text in ever new ways.

Literary interpretation argues that Revelation's language is not referential but polyvalent—expressive and evocative language. It does not appeal to logic but to the emotions. Interpreters, therefore, must acknowledge the ambiguity, openness, and indeterminacy of Revelation's literary vision and symbolic narrative. As a mythopoetic work, Revelation is not like a window to the world but is more like an onion or a rose with layers and layers of meaning. To destroy these layers of meaning by reducing them through referential correlation to only one definite meaning amounts to a serious misreading of the book. One could liken Revelation's symbolic narrative function to a prism refracting rich meaning in different and multiple ways.

Although multiple interpretations of a text are not only possible but inevitable, each interpretation of Revelation must nevertheless seek to make sense of the text's rich possibilities of meaning not only by foreclosing other readings but also by privileging one coherent reading. To achieve such a reading literary interpretations of Revelation tend to resort to platonic-idealist, existentialist, or archetypal approaches for articulating the deeper religious or theological meaning of the book. Such interpretations do not understand, for instance, the number 666 as a code referring to a particular first-century Roman ruler. Instead, they insist that the call for wisdom is not a call to decipher the number but to recognize its deeper meaning and significance. The number points to the archetypal conflict between the demonic and the divine.

Such a spiritualizing interpretation claims that Revelation does not speak about history but about timeless principles, inner spiritual realities, or psychological archetypes. For instance, interpreters suggest that Babylon embodies either the essence of urban civilization or the opposition between Babylon and the New Jerusalem. Others suggest that the female figures of Babylon and Jerusalem represent the archetype of *woman* as whore and virgin. Some argue either that the whole book reveals those basic principles by which God acts in history or that it depicts the ageless struggle between the forces of good and evil. Such a spiritualizing interpretation, however, risks mistaking a rose for an apricot when, in a psychological, platonic, essential, or existential reading, it reduces Revelation's multiple layers of meaning to a universalizing hard core of propositional truth. Rather than decoding either the images and symbols of Revelation or the whole book into logical, inferential, propositional language, one needs to trace how an image or symbol *works* within the overall composition of Revelation's mythological symbolization. For instance, Rev 11:8 states that the corpses of the two slain witnesses will lie in the street of the "great city" where their Lord was crucified. This great city is spiritually called "Sodom and Egypt." The "great city" is mentioned again in 16:19 in connection with Babylon. It is also mentioned in Rev 18:16, 18, 19 and explicitly identified in Rev 18:10 and 21 with Babylon/Rome. Rev 17:18 in turn identifies the great city with the harlot who has dominion over the kings of the earth and is drunk with the blood of the saints. She rides on a beast with seven heads. These heads are interpreted as the seven hills, an apparent allusion to the geographical location of the city of Rome.

B. A Rhetorical Analysis of Revelation

If the interplay, repetition, and elaboration of images and symbols in the total form-content configuration of Revelation engender the persuasive power of its imagination, then a *rhetorical* strategy of reading is called for. Again, by rhetorical I do not mean either "mere rhetoric" in a stylistic or propagandistic sense or "rhetorical figure" that does not correspond to fact or truth. Rather, I employ rhetoric here in the classical sense as the art and power of persuasion.

Rhetorical analysis seeks to explore the persuasive power of Revelation's symbolic language within the book's overall structure of meaning as well as within the rhetorical situation that is inscribed in the text and rooted in a particular sociohistorical matrix. The interpretation of Revelation attempted here seeks to develop a rhetorical strategy of reading which can integrate historical, literary, and theological analysis. Such a rhetorical analysis seeks to make sense of the text in terms of Revelation's overall literary configuration and symbolic universe as well as in terms of the book's power of persuasion both in its original and in its present-day rhetorical situation. This implies a shift in interpretative paradigm from an allegorical-spiritual, predictive-literalist, or historical-factual paradigm to a rhetorical-evocative paradigm that can do justice to the sociohistorical matrix as well as to the literary-dramatic character of the book.

In contradistinction to aesthetic and structuralist literary criticism, which focus on the literary form and deep structures of a text and conceptualize this analysis in universal terms, rhetorical discourse analysis stresses the importance of the speech context and sociohistorical matrix for understanding the persuasive force of an argumentation. It analyzes the persuasive power of a discourse not only in terms of rhetorical convention, literary style, and compositional arrangement, but also in terms of the speaker-audience relationship and the constraints placed on them by the sociocultural-religious location of the discourse. It analyzes Revelation as a moment of cultural exchange and theological argumentation between John and his audience that is determined by their common sociopolitical and cultural-religious situation.

Insofar as scholarly interest is shifting from its preoccupation with rhetoric as technical device, style, and ornamentation to rhetoric understood as sociopolitical persuasion, the scholar pays renewed attention to how arguments are constructed and how power is inscribed in biblical texts and to how interpretative discourse affects the social formation of which it is a part. Rhetorical analysis seeks not only to disclose the means with which authors or interpreters attempt to persuade or motivate their audience but also to trace the power-relations inscribed in the text and their functions in a particular rhetorical situation and sociohistorical location. Whenever I speak here of the author John and his communicative aims, therefore, I have in mind a *textualized* author, audience, and social location which are not identical with the *actual* participants and rhetorical practice of Revelation. The textualized rhetorical participants of Revelation and its sociohistorical rhetorical situation, however, should not be understood in purely ideological fictive terms that are totally abstracted from the actual sociohistorical situation and participants in Revelation's "first" production.

Classical theory of rhetoric addresses three types of speech—*judicial* (accusation-defense), *deliberative* (persuasion-dissuasion), and *epideictic* (praise and blame)—which are oriented toward three distinct social situations with different suasive occasions and rhetorical purposes. Judicial or forensic rhetoric functions like accusation and defense in a court of law; deliberative or advisory rhetoric fosters deliberation in a political assembly; and epideictic or ceremonial rhetoric has its place in civil ceremony and individual celebration. Whereas forensic rhetoric ponders past action and deliberative rhetoric considers future action, ceremonial speech performs present action. Insofar as the epideictic discourse seeks to praise, it is ethical both in topic and affective purpose. A ceremonial speaker invokes a certain set of ethical values that are embodied in the person praised in order to intensify the adherence of the audience to these values.

When one sets out to construct a rhetorical discourse (i.e., invention), the heuristic stage of preparation requires that one decide not only on the subject to be elaborated and the position to be taken but also on the suasive tenor and goal of the rhetorical intervention, which often requires a mixing of genres. According to classical rhetoric, the persuasive power of an argument is determined by *ethos, pathos,* and *pistis.* Both ethos and pathos are expected to be at work throughout the entire speech. Ethos is especially important at the beginning of the speech, whereas pathos unfolds primarily at the end of the discourse.

Issues that are engaged by rhetoric pertain to social and political matters that are debatable. Traditional views, cultural conventions, and established customs—the ways in which people view their world—are decisive in articulating persuasive arguments. Such arguments are supported by commonly held perspectives and beliefs which are called *pisteis* or "proofs." The discussion of such proofs addresses strategies for crafting a given argument and the kinds of material to be chosen. Three kinds of data (*paradeigma*) were generally listed: the example taken from a known case in history, the analogy derived from the world of customary behavior, and the mythos which created an imaginative world. All three were considered as proofs and not just as illustrations.

These categories and guidelines of classical rhetoric may, however, not be misconstrued as fixed containers or unchanging molds into which the text must be pressed. Rather than definite prescriptive structures, they are tools for analyzing the persuasive power of a text. Rhetorical discourse is not simply a question of technique and trope, but it engages substantive theo-ethical matters of power. Rhetoric as discourse is inseparable from the sociopolitical realities of its production.

Debates in public democratic assemblies, arguments about the merits of a lawsuit, and hymnic compositions celebrating gods or heroes are all clearly determined by the pragmatic sociopolitical situation that has generated them. A critical rhetorical analysis of Revelation seeks to trace its ideological practices and persuasive goals and to identify the literary means by which they are achieved. Discourse analysis of Revelation understands rhetoric not as mere ornamentation and empty style but as the art of persuasion. It must therefore concern itself with reconstructing both Revelation's rhetorical world of vision and the rhetorical and sociopolitical situations in which this imagery can be understood to have developed as an active and fitting response.

A rhetorical strategy of reading, therefore, seeks to analyze the text of Revelation as discursive interaction among the sociopolitical locations of its author, audience, and rhetorical situation. Such an interpretive practice that seeks to trace the inscribed politics of the text has its social location in communities that struggle for political, cultural, and religious change. In order to comprehend the visionary rhetoric of Revelation and the persuasive power of its vision I will discuss in the following sections: first, the paradox of Revelation's genre, since the book is written as a circular, open-letter speech to be heard in the Christian assembly, but it utilizes the language of apocalyptic symbol and myth rather than logical reasoning; second, the book's stylistic phrasing, the cultural conventions, theological traditions, and generic *topoi* on which the author draws for his proofs (*pisteis*); and third, Revelation's overall composition, symbolic arrangement, and dramatic structure.

1. The Generic Tenor of Revelation

Readers comprehend the meaning of a writing not only by interpreting its actual words and content but also by paying attention to what sort or type of writing they have before them. For instance, the meaning of the same words, phrases, and figures is different if they are read as the punch line of a joke, as a report in a business letter, or as a line in a hymn. Such a pragmatic notion of genre likens its function more to a musical key rather than to a preexisting form and independent schema. Rhetorical interpretation understands genre neither as something that is inherent in the text nor as a theoretical model into which texts must fit but as a heuristic, explanatory tool for unlocking the meaning of a text. For instance, interpreters wil! define the literary genre of Revelation and thereby read the book differently depending on whether they stress its apocalyptic features, its letter frame, its claim to be the words of prophecy, or its rhetorical elements. Rather than favoring one type of literary feature over the other, a rhetorical analysis seeks to identify generic tenors that help us to understand the book.

The literary definition of the genre apocalypse in general and that of Revelation in particular is still highly controverted and widely discussed. John's work is known either by its first Greek word as *Apocalypse* or by its Latin equivalent as *Revelation*. This title is derived from the book's opening statement: "This is the revelation [*apokalypsis*] God gave to Jesus Christ, that he may show his servants what must happen very soon" (Rev 1:1). While John claims that he wrote down what he saw and heard in his heavenly visions, scholars generally agree that the style and content of his work utilize Jewish apocalyptic tradition and convention. Revelation employs stock images, conventional *topoi* or places, scriptural figures, and proofs, as well as literary techniques developed in apocalyptic literature.

Yet the opening of Revelation clearly marks the author's intention to write a revelatory prophetic letter addressed to seven churches in western Asia Minor. The epistolary frame, which also reappears at the end of the book (Rev 22:21), is patterned after the, by then, traditional "Pauline" letter form. The topic and content of this letter is *apokalypsis*—revelation, which, according to 1 Cor 14:6, is one of the gifts of the Spirit. The terms *apokalypsis* and *apokalyptein* rarely appear in the Common Testament (Hebrew Bible or Old Testament). In Christian writings, they appear exclusively in Pauline and post-Pauline literature expressing visionary and ecstatic experience. The Pauline provenance of this notion is underlined by the fact that the expression "revelation of Jesus Christ" occurs only in this tradition. Yet scholars over-look this communicative designation of Revelation's genre as belonging to Pauline literature when they maintain that not only the book's style but also its genre is determined by Jewish apocalypticism.

Since the last century, the first word of Revelation, *apokalypsis,* has been used to characterize a whole group of Jewish and Christian writings which had flourished between 200 B.C.E. and 300 C.E. Examples of such apocalyptic literature include Daniel in the Common Testament and 4 Ezra (2 Esdr 3–14), which belongs to the so-called Apocrypha appended to most English editions of the Bible. Such Jewish apocalyptic writings include, among others, 1 and 2 Enoch, 2 and 3 Baruch, the Apocalypse of Abraham, and some writings from Qumran. In Christian Scriptures, we find not only apocalyptic sections (e.g., the so-called Synoptic apocalypse, Mark 13 par., or 2 Thess 2), but also basic apocalyptic categories and perspectives. Without question, Reve-lation belongs to this type of ancient literature.

Although Revelation's classification as apocalyptic literature is widely ac-cepted, such a generic delineation is often misapprehended as theological evaluation rather than understood as literary classification. As so-called apoca-lyptic literature, Revelation is often deemed not to be a Christian prophetic work but is seen as a Jewish work that is only slightly Christianized and that contributes little to our understanding of early Christian life, community, and theology. If, however, the classification "apocalyptic" is to be understood not as a literary container or a theological qualification but as a rhetorical prac-tice, then it is important to pay attention to the apocalyptic fashion in which Revelation is written.

One of the first comprehensive literary expressions of apocalyptic rhetoric appears in the book of Daniel, which was written in response to the religious persecution of Antiochus IV (ca. 165 B.C.E.). The crisis at the heart of Dan-iel's apocalyptic vision is a crisis of theodicy created by the contradiction between Israel's experience of suffering and its self-understanding as the cho-sen people of God. Despite all evidence to the contrary, this literature asserts that God remains in control and will soon intervene. Like Daniel, apocalyptic literature in general is often read as revelatory "crisis literature." Such a definition of apocalyptic writings underlines the rhetorical character of this type of literature.

The overall religious perspective of apocalyptic literature is eschatologi-cal—that is, it is concerned with the end of the world or the state of the soul after death. The apocalyptic frame of mind asserts that this age is under the power of evil and that the wicked therefore prosper and the righteous suffer. Yet this age will soon come to an end through the intervention of God. This end will be a catastrophe of cosmic proportions instigated by demonic and angelic forces. Before the end, a period of extreme tribulation will occur. After the cataclysm, a new salvation will appear via a mediator. Some apocalyptic writers expect the messianic reign of bliss and happiness for the elect on earth before the final cataclysm (messianism or chiliasm).

Scholars specify the literary genre and stylistic features of apocalyptic writings in different ways. The following features are considered as typical for apocalypses: The author receives a secret revelation and instructions to write it down. Such revelation is imparted in dreams, visions, auditions, and interpretations by a heavenly guide or angelic interpreter. It involves another, heavenly world and envisions eschatological salvation; however, the visionary apparatus represents literary technique rather than a transcript of ecstatic experience.

Apocalyptic literature is essentially a written rather than an oral literature. It invites the audience to participate in the visions and auditions of the seer. It utilizes conventional imagery and traditional symbolism as a shared code to allow mutual understanding between seer and reader. Major literary techniques include periodization of history and pseudonymity (i.e., the reception of the revelation is attributed to a figure of the past). These literary techniques of periodization and pseudonymity allow the author to present past history as an accurate prediction of future events. The mysterious character of apocalyptic literature is achieved through fantastic symbolizations and mythical imagery that must be read on two levels. Numbers do not designate quantifiable amounts but have symbolic value. Similarly, colors signify symbolic meaning—for instance: red is the color of war and fighting; white is the color of victory or of heavenly being; and pale is the color of death.

Apocalyptic language functions not as predictive-descriptive language but rather as mythological-imaginative language. It is not like a cloak which can be stripped down to its theological essence or principle. It does not appeal to our logical faculties but to our imagination and emotions. It is mythological-fantastic language—stars fall from heaven; the world becomes as a palace with three stories: heaven, earth, and underworld; animals speak, dragons spit fire, a lion is a lamb, and angels or demons engage in warfare.

Apocalyptic literature speaks about the past, present, and future in mythological language and images. Daniel, for example, has a vision of four wild beasts emerging from the sea that are later identified as four great kings (chap. 7). The bizarre and terrifying features of these beasts indicate that they are not conceived as real beasts but as mythological symbolizations. The first beast, for instance, is likened to a lion with eagle's wings, while the third is compared to a leopard with four heads and four bird wings on its flanks

(Dan 7:4-7). Thus in apocalyptic literature, world empires become beasts, nations are symbolized by birds, and serpents start to speak. Apocalyptic literature is surrealistic, fantastic literature.

Apocalyptic literature, therefore, could be compared to the future-oriented genre of science fiction that constructs the future out of the experience and fears of people in the present. Anyone who enjoys the tales and future projections of science-fiction writers, however, would readily agree that this literature does not predict what is going to happen but illuminates our present situation by projecting current hopes and fears into the future. It utilizes our knowledge of today for envisioning future possibilities.

A pragmatic rhetorical understanding that does not understand genre as a preexisting pattern inherent in the text but as a scholarly construction for classificatory purposes does not need to determine the genre of Revelation as either an apocalypse, or as an open letter, or as an early Christian prophetic work. Rather its readings can explore these literary forms as rhetorical strategies of the author. All three modes of rhetoric—deliberative, forensic, and ceremonial—appear to have shaped parts of Revelation. Revelation's epistolary framework and its calls to deliberation and decision function as deliberative rhetoric in the assembly of the community. Its indictments, warnings, and narrative symbolization of divine judgments, as well as its promises and depictions of reward and punishment, qualify it as forensic rhetoric; whereas its visionary depictions of the heavenly "liturgy" and its hymnic praises identify it as ceremonial rhetoric. To decide for one over and against the other would not enhance but diminish our readings.

2. Stylistic Phrasing:
Language and Imagery

Rhetorical style influences an author's selection of words, figures of speech, metaphors, and images. It also affects narrative transitions and clarity of speech. Rhetorical style is not merely an aesthetic means. It provides also a clue to the *ethos* as well as to the trustworthiness and authority of the speaker. At the same time, it is also a primary means of creating *pathos*, that is, the desired effect upon the audience.

Like apocalyptic literature in general, Revelation seeks to make sense of the world and the present time either in terms of the transcendent or of the future or in terms of both. John achieves this by picturing the heavenly world and the eschatological future with the help of knowledge and language gleaned from past and present experience in this world. Like other apocalyptic authors, John describes the future in terms of the knowledge available to him in the present. He speaks about heavenly or demonic realities that are not commonly available to human experience and knowledge. In order to do so, he utilizes the human language and imagery known in the mythology, traditions, and scientific knowledge of his own time.

John searches the Scriptures for allusions and associations that will provide a sacred language for his narrative symbolization. He probes for typologies and exemplary figures to serve as paradigms for his rhetorical composition and as rhetorical proofs for Revelation's world of vision. For instance, John's depiction of God's judgment on those who oppress God's people in the seven trumpet and bowl series is modeled after the Exodus narrative and its reception in the Wisdom of Solomon. The Exodus pattern gives shape to Revelation's depiction of oppression and redemption in these judgment visions.

In a similar fashion, Julia Esquivel employs as "traditional" language the imagery and language of Revelation which is enriched by textual allusions to the Hebrew Bible. Her narrative poem "Thanksgiving Day in the United States" utilizes Rev 17–18 as her literary model and symbolic language source.* Since the poem is too long to reproduce here in its entirety, I have selected excerpts to illustrate my point:

> In the third year of the massacres
> by Lucas and the other coyotes
> against the poor of Guatemala
> I was led by the Spirit into the desert

> And on the eve
> of Thanksgiving Day
> I had a vision of Babylon:
> The city sprang forth arrogantly
> from an enormous platform
> of dirty smoke produced
> by motor vehicles, machinery
> and contamination from smokestacks.

> It was as if all the petroleum
> from a violated earth
> was being consumed
> by the Lords of capital
> and was slowly rising
> obscuring the face
> of the Sun of Justice
> and the Ancient of Days. . . .

*Julia Esquivel, from *Threatened with Resurrection: Prayers and Poems from an Exiled Guatemalan* (Elgin: The Brethren Press, 1982), 79–91.

Each day false prophets
invited the inhabitants
of the Unchaste City
to kneel before the idols
of gluttony,
money,
and death:
Idolaters from all nations
were being converted to the American Way of Life. . . .

The Spirit told me
in the River of death
flows the blood of many peoples
sacrificed without mercy
and removed a thousand times from their lands,
the blood of Kekchis, of Panzos,
of blacks from Haiti, of Guaranis from Paraguay,
of the peoples sacrificed for "development"
in the Trans-Amazonic strip,
the blood of the Indians' ancestors
who lived on these lands, of those who
even now are kept hostage in the Great Mountain
and on the Black Hills of Dakota
by the guardians of the beast. . . .

My soul was tortured like this
for three and a half days
and a great weariness weighed upon my breast.
I felt the suffering of my people very deeply!

Then in tears, I prostrated myself
and cried out: "Lord, what can we do? . . .
Come to me, Lord, I wish to die among my people!"
Without strength, I waited for the answer.
After a long silence
and a heavy obscurity
The One who sits on the throne
to judge the nations
spoke in a soft whisper
in the secret recesses of my heart:

You have to denounce their idolatry
in good times and in bad.
Force them to hear the truth
for what is impossible to humans
is possible for God.

This poem clearly utilizes but does not reproduce the language and imagery of Revelation in order to express a contemporary apocalyptic world of vision. The translator of the poem used many annotations for explaining to the reader who is not familiar with colonial history the names, images, and references which the poet uses. In a similar fashion, exegetes must explain the numerous allusions and references of Revelation to diverse tradition and materials contemporary with John that in all likelihood would have been familiar to the first readers of the book.

Like Julia Esquivel's poem, Revelation is written for the sake of prophetic interpretation and motivation. As a Christian seer, the author gives not simply moral injunctions and prescriptive admonitions, but he constructs a symbolic universe and "plausibility structure." He does so in order to speak to the experience and predicament of Christians of his own time who are a powerless minority vis-à-vis the dominant majority power of their own culture. Therefore, he employs socioeconomic language and political-mythological imagery.

In creating this mythological symbolization, John does not freely invent his images and symbols but derives them from Jewish and Greco-Roman literature and tradition. By working with associations and allusions to very divergent mythic and religious-political traditions, he appeals to the imagination of his audience. He does not invent his images and myth but employs them utilizing apocalyptic language as traditional language.

Readers can trace how the author composes his language and imagery by comparing his text with that of the Hebrew Bible, which he has utilized as his language reservoir. Although John knows how to write proper Greek, he writes the whole book in a Hebraizing idiom that gives its language a hieratic, traditional character. Moreover, he never quotes or exegetes the Hebrew Bible or any of his other sources but uses them as "language" and "models."

A careful look at the inaugural vision (1:10-20) may demonstrate why one is justified in calling Revelation a "literary vision." It is impossible to picture or draw this vision, for its images and symbols function more like words and sentences in a composition. One could say that the author constructs his sentences and paragraphs with symbols and images derived from the Hebrew Bible and apocalyptic Jewish literature rather than with abstract concepts and theological statements.

A comparison of the figure in Daniel 10 with that of Christ in Revelation 1 indicates that John works in an associative-anthological literary fashion insofar as he closely follows the text of Daniel 10 but also differs from it in several instances. These differences point to the emphases which Revelation stresses. Through these explicit changes, the text stresses Christ's royal/priestly character. This emphasis is not found in the Daniel text that served as John's basic literary pattern for the composition of this vision.

Yet, Revelation's language and images are derived not only from Hebrew-Jewish but also from Babylonian, Zoroastrian, Greco-Roman, and Asian mythological traditions. Although these were readily available and unconsciously present to the original recipients of the book, they are difficult for modern readers to understand. For instance, the depiction of the One in Human Likeness as holding the "keys to Death and Hades" (1:18b) evokes the image of the goddess Hecate. This goddess is the primary mythological figure who, in the Hellenistic world, was believed to hold the keys to the gates of Hades. During the Greco-Roman period, Hecate was very popular in Asia Minor and was celebrated as universal sovereign of the cosmos.

How John employs such traditional mythological language can be illustrated especially with reference to chapter 12. The myth of the queen of heaven with the divine child was internationally known at the time of John. Variations of it are found in Babylonia, Egypt, Greece, and Asia Minor. The elements of this myth—the goddess with the divine child, the great red dragon and his enmity to mother and child, and their protection—are also incorporated in Revelation 12. Some features of this myth appear also in the Roman imperial cult. For instance, a coin of Pergamum portrays the goddess Roma with the imperial child.

People worshiped Roma, the queen of heaven, as the mother of the gods in the cities of Asia Minor. Her oldest temple stood in Smyrna. Her imperial child was celebrated as the "world's savior" and as sun-god Apollo. Such an allusion to the imperial cult and to the goddess Roma is probably intended in Revelation 12, since the "woman clothed with the sun" clearly is the anti-image of Babylon, which in all likelihood represents Rome and its allies in chapters 17 and 18. John reinterprets this ancient myth in terms of Jewish expectations. The stress on the travail of the woman is not found in Greco-Roman myth but is inspired by the prophetic image of Israel-Zion in the messianic times.

The tensive multivalent symbol of the "woman clothed with the sun" has sparked very different interpretations. Scholars have identified her as representing Israel as the heavenly or earthly church, or as Mary, the mother of Jesus. If one analyzes the place of the image of "the Queen of Heaven" and its relationships in the symbol system of Revelation, one recognizes that it functions as antitype to that of "Babylon, the Great" and as prototype to that of the New Jerusalem coming down from heaven like a bride adorned for her husband (19:7ff; 21:2,9ff). As a heavenly and eschatological figure, the symbol "woman" signifies not only the protection and salvation of the people of God but also the future of a renewed world.

The figure of the dragon, serpent, crocodile, or sea monster is also familiar from both ancient mythology and the Hebrew Bible. In Hebrew-Jewish writings the dragon frequently serves as a symbol for the oppressor nation. Such oppressor nations include Egypt (Ps 74:14) and its ruler, Pharaoh (Ezek 32:3ff), Syria, and Babylon (Isa 27:1). In Daniel, the dragon symbolizes the last great antidivine nation and the ruler opposing Israel (7:1-7). In this traditional symbolic context, the red dragon is immediately recognized as the ultimate foe of the people of God.

By working with associations and with allusions to divergent mythic and religious-political traditions, Revelation seeks to appeal to the imagination of people steeped in Jewish as well as Greco-Roman culture and religion. John achieves the rhetorical power of his work by taking traditional symbols and mythological images out of their original contexts and by placing them like mosaic stones into the new literary composition of his symbolic narrative movement.

Revelation, therefore, must be read and contemplated as a symphony of images if one wants to experience the book's full emotional impact. Literary and historical analyses can deepen the book's persuasive mythological *pathos* but can not replace it. An analysis of Revelation's sources and traditions helps to elucidate the possible meanings of Revelation's images, but such an analysis does not explain them. Their meaning cannot be derived from the tradition but only from their present position within the overall symbolic framework and rhetorical narrative of the book.

The strength of Revelation's mythic symbolization and world of vision thus lies primarily in neither its theological reasoning nor its historical information but in the evocative, persuasive power of its symbolic language compelling imaginative participation. The multivalent images and tensive symbols of Revelation elicit emotions, feelings, and convictions that cannot, and should not, be fully conceptualized. Attempts to express Revelation's images and metaphors in propositional, logical, factual language rob them of their power of persuasion. Thus the mythopoetic language of Revelation resembles poetry and drama. Any adequate exploration and comprehension of Revelation must appreciate the persuasive power and evocative musicality of the book, which was originally written as a dramatic poem to be read aloud and heard in the worship gatherings of the Asian communities.

3. Rhetorical Arrangement and Composition

In rhetorical theory, *arrangement* refers to the ordering of the material by the speaker, the choices concerning sequence, development of subthemes, and elaboration of certain points. Skilled authors are expected to make their outlines invisible so that the composition will appear to unfold by itself. That John is such a skilled writer is demonstrated by the fact that numerous scholarly outlines have been prepared for the book. Following decisions about the arrangement, the last two steps in the preparation of a speech attend to the props for *memorizing* and techniques for the actual *delivery* which are incorporated in the work.

The fact that the apocalyptic visions of Revelation are communicated in the form of an open letter to seven communities in Asia Minor discloses the rhetorical function of Revelation. The author gives clear instructions for the book's oratorical *delivery*. John is told to write down the "words of prophecy" (1:11) which are "the revelation of Jesus Christ." His book of prophecy is to be read aloud in the assembly of the community so that its readers and hearers will receive eschatological blessings (1:3). Moreover, as the book closes, the audience is threatened with eschatological disaster and warned not to add to or take away from the words of this prophetic book (22:18-19).

The mythopoetic persuasive power of Revelation's world of vision can best be experienced when one hears the book read aloud in its entirety. Its archaic, Hebraizing language; the repetition of sounds and formulas; the wealth of its colors, voices, and image associations: all these work together to persuade the hearer of the author's vision. This dramatic and symbolic character of Revelation defies exact analysis and definite interpretation. It would therefore be a serious mistake to reduce the visionary rhetoric of Revelation to abstract system or to moral argument. Rather, one has to approach the book in the same manner in which one would approach a work of art. If one seeks to appreciate a symphony, for example, one must listen to the whole work in order to grasp the full impact of its total composition—its tonal colors, musical forms, motifs, and relationships. Only after one has listened to the work as a whole can one go on and analyze the elements and details of its composition and study the techniques employed by its composer.

Likewise, Revelation can be fully appreciated only when analyzed in its entirety as a literary-rhetorical arrangement, because each vision and symbol takes its import in relation to Revelation's overall symbolic configuration. Revelation's poetic-rhetorical vision exists within the overall framework of an apocalyptic myth. The notion of "mythological symbolization" may help readers to conceive of Revelation as a cohesive body of images and symbols creating an apocalyptic myth that has persuasive power. This notion also allows one to break down the mythological symbolization of Revelation into its component symbols and images and to understand individual images and metaphors within the overall literary composition and dramatic structure of the book.

Nevertheless, Revelation's composition is not encyclopedic but dramatic, due to the author's literary techniques and compositional skills that integrate the various traditions and symbols into the literary movement of the work. Such literary techniques function at the same time as rhetorical markers that help the auditor to hold the structure and key images of Revelation in memory. Such rhetorical markers are, for instance, the technique of numbering, the locators of image and place, and the introduction of three scrolls or books (1:11; 5:1; 10:1), each corresponding to discrete actions.

Techniques of composition. The author achieves a unified dramatic composition primarily by using a common stock of symbols and images. Individual visions do not contain an exclusive set of images. On the contrary, the main symbols and images appear throughout the work (e.g., the symbol of the throne or the image of prostration). The author also achieves a unified narrative structure by employing image clusters and symbol associations that reinforce each other. Like a musical motif, they connect the individual visions with each other (e.g., the image of the throne achieves its full impact and "volume" by its allusions and associations with other symbols of imperial power and reign). Further techniques promoting literary integration include: preannouncements (e.g., the promises to the victor at the end of the seven messages find elaboration in chaps. 21f); cross-references (some christological characteristics of the inaugural vision in 1:10-20 are repeated not only in chaps. 2f but also in 14:14ff and 19:11ff); and contrasts (e.g., the great Babylon in chaps. 17f versus the New Jerusalem of chaps. 12 and 21f).

Another primary means by which to achieve an interwoven texture and unified composition consists in the author's use of numbers and numerical patterns. Structuring numerical component forms are the four "seven cycles" of the message and plague visions, the two book visions symbolizing a new prophetic commission, and the two visions of Christ with the sword, the symbol of judgment (1:13ff; 19:11ff). The seven cycles in turn are further structured into groups of four and three. The author's numerical interweaving of visions combines a cyclic form of repetition with a continuous forward movement.

This method of composition makes Revelation end-oriented rather than cyclic or encyclopedic. The forward surge of the narrative, however, is slowed by visionary interludes of eschatological protection and salvation. By interrupting the patterns of continuous narrative and cyclic repetition through the insertion of these anticipatory visions of salvation, the author underlines the interrelation between the present situation of harassment and the eschatological future of salvation. At the same time, he conveys structurally through this composition that the eschatological future gives meaning to the present situation and struggle.

Very crucial for understanding Revelation is the literary technique of *intercalation*, or sandwiching, insofar as it makes a diagramming of the successive sections and narrative development almost impossible. John uses this method of intercalation in the following way: He narrates two episodes or uses two symbols or images which essentially belong together. Between these two sections or symbols (A and A'), he then inserts another (B). In doing so he compels the reader to see the whole text as an indivisible whole. For example, he introduces the seven-trumpet series with the following inclusion:

A: "Next I saw seven trumpets being given . . ." (8:2);
B: "Another angel who had a golden censer . . ." (8:3-5);
A': "The seven angels that had the seven trumpets . . ." (8:6ff).

Many sections of Revelation display such a structure and form of inclusion or nestling.

The technique of interlocking or interlacing combines the ABA' pattern and the interlude. The author inserts into a given narrative sequence a section or vision which clearly belongs also to the following section of the narrative. For instance, the section 10:1—11:14 constitutes an interlude before the opening of the seventh trumpet and at the same time clearly remains a part of chapters 12–14. The method of intercalation is a great obstacle to a Western mindset because we customarily divide a text into sections that follow each other in a logical-linear fashion. The form of exegetical commentary follows this Western thought-pattern.

The author of Revelation does not separate the narrative structure into clearcut segments or logical sequences, but he joins individual visions and cycles together by interweaving them with each other through the techniques of intercalation and inclusion. Although scholars usually look for the "dividing marks" in the outline of Revelation, it seems more fruitful to concentrate on the "joints" that connect the different cycles of visions; therefore, I will not arrange the commentary along the traditional chapter divisions but will elaborate whole clusters of visions.

Narrative movement. That one can find almost as many outlines and structurations of Revelation as there are scholars studying the book speaks for the rhetorical skill of the author. Since modern readers are trained in linear-logical thinking, we expect a linear-temporal sequence of visions. Anticipatory interludes and hymns, apparent repetitions, and the repeated announcement that the end is here confuse and startle us. Commentators have therefore argued for the cyclic nature of Revelation's narrative but have overlooked the forward movement of the narrative. Insofar as the promises of the seven messages recur without exception in the last section of the book, the narrative's forward movement progresses from promise to fulfillment.

To complicate matters, the narrative's forward movement does not follow a linear-logical or linear-temporal development. Rather, it can best be envisioned as a conical spiral moving from the present to the eschatological future. Paradoxically, this forward movement of the narrative leads not to a flight into a utopian future but anchors the reader in the present of the seven communities. Moreover, this spiraling literary vision and composition of Revelation moves within the boundaries of an epistolary framework that in early Christianity had become typical for the prophetic pastoral letter. In addition, exhortations, beatitudes, and warnings relate the apocalyptic images and visions to the present experience of the Christian community.

If the forward movement of the narrative as well as the concentric pattern of the epistolary inclusion determine the structure of Revelation, then any proposed outline of the book must take note of this compositional tension. The component parts and concentric movements of Revelation's surface structure can be sketched in the following way (Roman numerals indicate explicitly numbered seven-series):

A.   **1:1-8: Prologue and Epistolary Greeting**
    1:1-3: Title
    1:4-6: Greetings
    1:7-8: Motto

B.   **1:9—3:22: Rhetorical Situation in the Cities of Asia Minor**
    1:9-10: Author and Situation
    1:11-20: Prophetic Inaugural Vision
  I.   2:1—3:22: Prophetic Messages to Seven Communities

C.   **4:1—9:21; 11:15-19: Opening the Sealed Scroll:**
    Exodus Plagues
    4:1—5:14: Heavenly Court and Sealed Scroll
  II. 6:1—8:1: Cosmic Plagues: Seven Seals
  III. 8:2—9:21; 11:15-19: Cosmic Plagues: Seven Trumpets

D.   **10:1—15:4: The Bitter-Sweet Scroll: "War" against**
    the Community
    10:1—11:14: Prophetic Commissioning
    12:1—14:5: Prophetic Interpretation
    14:6—15:4: Eschatological Liberation

C'.   **15:5—19:10: Exodus from the Oppression of Babylon/Rome**
  IV. 15:5—16:21: Cosmic Plagues: Seven Bowls
    17:1-18: Rome and Its Power
    18:1—19:10: Judgment of Rome

B'. **19:11—22:9: Liberation from Evil and God's World-City**
   19:11—20:15: Liberation from the Powers of Evil
   21:1-8: The Liberated World of God
   21:9—22:9: The Different Cosmopolis of God

A'. **22:10-21: Epilogue and Epistolary Frame**
   22:10-17: Revelatory Sayings
   22:18-21: Epistolary Conclusion

This concentric *ABCDC'B'A'* structure occurs also in Jewish and Greco-Roman literature and art. It indicates that the whole book is conceived in the form of an inclusion that is comparable to a Russian doll in which several other dolls are nestled. Yet as pointed out already, Revelation's narrative is not static but dynamic. It is best envisioned as a conic spiral moving from the present to the eschatological future.

Revelation's development of symbol and thought could also be said to unfold in a prismatic rather than sequential fashion. Or, Revelation's narrative could be likened to that of a dramatic motion picture whose individual scenes portray the same persons or action each time from a different angle or perspective, while simultaneously adding some new insight to the whole. Or, it might be compared to a musical composition that varies its main themes in different ways, each variation enhancing and moving the total composition.

For me, Sonia Delaunay's expressionist paintings capture best the type of development of symbol and movement in Revelation. Her picture *Rhythm*, for instance, contains a number of differently colored circles or half-circles from which radiate lines of colors like light splintered by a prism. The picture is not static; rather, its lines indicate a momentum within the circles of color similar to that of a revolving planet. While the evolving circles of color evoke simultaneity, the contrasting colors create a sense of light and spiraling movement.

One must keep in mind, however, that John develops this dynamic composition of Revelation in the interest of persuading his audience to accept his prophetic interpretation of their situation. His work seeks to persuade and compel readers to a certain Christian praxis, one of resistance and hope. Its compositional motion could be likened to a journey that moves the audience from alienation through commitment to liberation. The first part of the journey is *the way in.* It states the primary conditions in terms of which the starting point of the journey is to be localized or specified in time. This function is fulfilled by the first section, the seven messages of Revelation (1:9—3:22).

The next part within the journey metaphor is the definite *pushing off from shore* and the certainty *of being underway.* On a particular journey one can be underway for varying periods of time. Chapters 4–9, culminating in the seventh trumpet, take the audience on the way of the journey which opened up with the death, resurrection, and exaltation of Christ.

Eventually, one has to arrive at the innermost *heart of the matter*. Here one arrives at knowledge and perception of the tensions (e.g., pollution, psychosis, civil disorder, class conflicts), that is, at the exigency of the rhetorical situation that is symbolized and explored. Chapters 10–14 and 15:2-4 represent structurally this prophetic "withinness of withinness" of the symbolic drama of Revelation.

From this point on, the audience is *returning* and goes back to the starting point, but with a difference which is constituted by an emotional or intellectual commitment, a *separating out* that happens in Rev 15:5—19:10. This last part of the dramatic action completes the journey and the motivation process. The journey is complete when the passion (persecution and suffering) has been transformed into a utopic assertion. The book closes with such a final assertion in 19:11—22:5. In taking his audience on such a dramatic-rhetorical journey, John seeks to move them to control their fear, to renew their commitment, and to sustain their vision.

PART TWO

COMMENTARY

A. Prologue and Epistolary Greeting
Revelation 1:1-8

Introduction

In order to understand Revelation's multivalent imagery, one must pay careful attention to its rhetorical composition. Much like the prophetic books of the Hebrew Bible, Revelation begins with an elaborate introduction divided into three parts: Like the book of Amos (1:1-2), so also Revelation is prefaced with a title (1:1-3) and a motto (1:7-8), which announce both the content and the perspective of the book. The epistolary greeting inserted into the traditional form of the prophetic prologue resembles that of the Pauline Letters (1:4-6). This carefully composed introduction thus formally characterizes Revelation as a work of prophetic rhetoric that functions like an open pastoral letter addressed to seven Christian churches in Asia Minor (modern-day Turkey). The careful elaboration of the prologue as well as the injunctions to write (1:11, 19) indicate that the author understands his work as a literary prophecy.

Revelation 1:1-3
Title

The title of Revelation concisely describes its contents as well as the authority which impels its chain of communication. This "headline" identifies the book both as a "revelation [*apokalypsis*] of Jesus Christ" and as the "words of prophecy." The Greek word for revelation appears only here, where it seems to function as a title for the whole work. One should note, however, that the original title of the book is "revelation" or "apocalypse" *not* of John but of Jesus Christ. The popular title "Revelation of John" was added only later when the book was accepted into the canon. It seems to be derived from the first three verses and was probably formulated by analogy with the titles of other Jewish and Christian apocalypses attributed to great figures of the past: for example, Abraham, Ezra, Baruch, or Peter.

As distinct from other Jewish and Christian apocalypses, Revelation does not claim the authority of John but the authority of Jesus Christ. In a similar fashion, Paul insists that he did not receive the gospel from human authorities but has learned it "only through a revelation of Jesus Christ" (Gal 1:12ff). The full title "Jesus Christ" occurs only in the title Rev 1:1-2 and in the epistolary greeting of Rev 1:5, and it is not found elsewhere in the book. The author seems to refer deliberately to the Pauline linguistic and theological understandings of apocalypse that become almost synonymous with the gift of prophecy (1 Corinthians 14). He can, therefore, alternately characterize the book as "revelation of Jesus Christ" and as "the words of prophecy."

The words of prophecy come from God who gave them to Jesus Christ who in turn gave them, through an angel, to the Christian prophets and especially to the seer John. Thus Revelation is authorized not by John but by God. The words of prophecy promise that eschatological judgment and salvation are imminent: "The last time is at hand"—that which, according to God's plan, has to take place in the immediate future is revealed to the prophets. Although the expression "servants" may characterize all Christians, it probably designates in this context Christian prophets, since according to Amos 3:7, God does nothing without revealing it to the servants of God, the prophets. Now, through Jesus Christ, God reveals the end times to the Christian prophets. The ethos of Revelation is thus established in a double fashion, insofar as its authors are God and Jesus Christ and the words of prophecy are communicated through an angel and through John.

That this revelation is communicated by an angel is typical of traditional apocalyptic style. Moreover, that this prophecy is not told but *signified*, or shown, likewise indicates apocalyptic style. Such literary apocalyptic style resembles that of poetry insofar as it does not seek to argue logically but to express its vision in literary symbols and images which appeal not only to the intellect but also to the emotions of the reader or hearer.

The first section of the prologue concludes with a beatitude, a blessing for those who read or hear the words of prophecy. This beatitude makes clear that Revelation is conceived as a rhetorical work to be recited in the assembly of the community. Anyone who has ever really listened to the whole book will agree that it comes to life only when read aloud to an audience. As we know from the Pauline literature and from the Didache, Christian prophets were generally expected to speak in the liturgical assembly of the congregation. John clearly hopes that his writing will function during his absence as such a prophetic utterance within the worship of the churches.

Revelation 1:4-6
Epistolary Greeting

For communicating the words of prophecy to the churches in Asia Minor, John writes his work in the form of the Pauline epistle, which by then was already a traditional form. In a way similar to the opening greetings of the

Pauline Letters, the epistolary introduction mentions the sender, John, and the recipients, the seven churches. Unlike other apocalypses, Revelation is thus not pseudonymous and does not locate its author as a person of the past. Rather, it assumes that he is well known to the recipients, since it mentions him by name only. Although ecclesiastical tradition has identified the author of Revelation with the apostle John, such an assumption is not tenable. Since Rev 21:14 speaks of the twelve apostles as figures of the past, its author must be a different John from the apostle John. We therefore no longer know who the author of Revelation actually was—yet he must have been well known to the churches in Asia Minor since he does not require any further introduction or authorization.

Like Paul, John replaces the standard Hellenistic greeting with the expression "grace and peace"; however, he greatly expands Paul's usual formula "from God, the Father, and the Lord Jesus Christ" by adding as another source the "seven spirits" and by characterizing Christ with three titles: Christ is the reliable eschatological witness. Christ is the inaugurator and representative of the new creation. Christ is the sovereign exercising full kingship and power. Grace and peace come from God, from the seven spirits, and from Jesus Christ, to whom the concluding doxology ascribes glory and power forever. The three christological titles derive from early Christian tradition, and they characterize Jesus Christ in relationship to the Christian community.

These three titles of Christ are paralleled in 1:6 by three statements about the activity of Christ that probably are derived from the early Christian baptismal tradition: Christ loves those whom he has redeemed. He has freed them from personal sins through his death. He has installed them as priestly representatives of the kingdom or empire of God, who is called "Father." The three honorary titles of Christ, the three predicative statements about Christ's activity, and the doxology together form a formal unity of praise; however, the connection of the three titles with the name "Jesus Christ" is grammatically incorrect. Moreover, the second title, "first-born of the dead," reflects traditional Christology as it is found in the hymn of Col 1:18 and in the Pauline Letters (Rom 8:29 and 1 Cor 15:20). It could, therefore, be possible that these titles together were derived from tradition. Insofar as the first and third titles reflect John's theology, it is more probable that these titles only contain traditional material and were formed as a unit by the author himself. The titles do not, therefore, represent an early Christian formula that refers to the death, resurrection, and exaltation of Christ. Instead, they express the author's own theological interest in emphasizing the relationship of Christ to the community.

The three titles of Christ are followed by three predicative statements about the activity of Christ. The participle style, the placement of the participles at the beginning of every clause, the parallelism of the three members, the switch from the personal pronoun *hymin* (you) to *hēmas* (we), and finally the doxology at the end of the unit: these give the impression that the whole is a hymnic formulation composed by the author or taken over from tradition. If the doxology were connected only by the author himself with the three predicative statements about the activity of Christ, then these statements could have originally formed a confessional formula which John crafted into a hymn of praise. John could have transformed the whole unit (the titles, the predicative statements, and the doxology) into a hymn of praise in order to make it parallel to the Pauline thanksgivings. Since the whole greeting has been written in the form of the Pauline letter prescript, this assumption becomes even more probable.

If the aorist tense in the three predicative statements about the activity of Christ reflects early Christian language and traditional material, it must be asked to which tradition this material belongs. A form-critical investigation would indicate that this material probably had its *Sitz im Leben* in the baptismal tradition. If that is the case, then John might have altered the first part of the statement in 1:5-6 from the past to the present tense. The aorist of the verb love (*agapein*) followed by the accusative is frequently found in early Christian pre-Pauline tradition (e.g., in Gal 2:20; 2 Thess 2.16; Eph 1:5-6; 2:4ff; and 5:25ff). This tradition can be characterized as baptismal. As Rev 3:9 indicates, John knows this tradition in which the aorist of *agapein* was used with the accusative. In contrast to the LXX (Septuagint) text of Isa 43:4, the author emphasizes the loving activity of Christ in the present (Rev 3:9 and 1:5). Even though the present time is full of tribulations for Christians, Christ's love is now with them.

The second member of the formula in Rev 1:5-6 refers to setting Christians free from their own sins through the blood of Christ. The use of the term blood (*haima*) in connection with forgiveness of sins is found very early. It is not only present in the tradition of the word about the cup in the Lord's Supper, but also in pre-Pauline formulas. The phrase "to him who has freed" (*lysanti* is preferable to the Greek variant *lousanti*) is used only here in the New Testament. It shares, however, its root with other expressions for redemption (*lytron, lytrousthai,* or *apolytrōsis*). These terms are used in connection with blood (*haima*) to denote "redemption" (Rom 3:24-26; Eph 1:7; Heb 9:12; 1 Pet 1:19). Whether they belong to the baptismal or to the eucharistic tradition is, however, a matter of debate. The textual variant "to him who has washed" (*lousanti*) could indicate that Rev 1:5 was very early understood as referring to baptism. Through his blood, Christ has set the baptized free from their own personal sins. Thus redemption is understood here in an anthropological sense as the liberation of those baptized from the evil actions and deeds of their past.

The third member of the formula in Rev 1:6 speaks about the installation of the redeemed "to kingship, to priests for God." The grammatically difficult Greek phrase *basileian hiereis* (the abstract singular *basileian* is placed together with the concrete plural *hiereis*) probably refers to a textual version of Exod 19:6 which is not found in the LXX. The verb "to make" (*poiein*), however, is found neither in this Exodus text nor in the New Testament parallel text of 1 Pet 2:9, where the LXX text of Exod 19:6 has been taken over. Since the verb *poiein* refers here to concrete persons who are given a new dignity, it should probably be translated in the sense of "investing" or "installing" someone. This usage of "to make" (*poiein*) in this sense is not found in classical Greek but in the LXX and in the New Testament. The phrase *kai epoiēsen* is so used in Mark 3:4-19, where it refers to the institution of the Twelve ("And *he appointed* twelve"), and in Acts 2:36, where it refers to the investiture of Jesus as Lord and Messiah by God. The closest parallel to Rev 1:6 is, however, found in 1 Sam 12:6 and in 1 Kgs 12:31 and 13:33-34, where the aorist form of this verb is also used in connection with the accusative of priests (*hiereis*). These Hebrew Bible texts emphasize that in the Northern Kingdom every member of the nation could be installed as a priest by Jeroboam and did not have to be a member of the priestly Levitical tribe. Thus Rev 1:6 maintains that Christ installed the redeemed to kingship, to be priests for God, the Father. The use of the aorist and the reference to Exod 19:6 (which is also found in 1 Pet 2:9 in a passage full of baptismal allusions) makes it probable that the third member of the statement about the activity of Christ belongs to a baptismal tradition.

In short, this analysis of Rev 1:5-6 indicates that all three statements about the activity of Christ represent formulary material which in all probability belonged to the early Christian baptismal tradition. In their traditional form, these three statements did not have the form of a hymn, as in the present context, but that of a confessional formula, which emphasized the loving activity of Christ at the beginning of Christian existence. This beginning in baptism is concretely explicated both as the liberation from their own sins by the death of Christ and as their investiture with the dignity and power of both kings and priests. By changing the first aorist to the present tense, the author stresses that Christ's love is now with those whom Christ has redeemed and installed with kingship to be priests for God.

Revelation 1:7-8
Motto

The prologue concludes with a prophetic announcement of Christ's coming (*parousia*) (1:7), which is followed by an explicit word of God (1:8). The prophetic announcement of the parousia indicates again how deeply the author is steeped in the Hebrew Bible as well as in early Christian traditions. John does not quote his sources but uses these traditions as a language resource for his own prophetic statements.

Revelation 1:7 seems to be a textual conflation of Dan 7:13 and Zech 12:10. This announcement shares its eschatological tenor with the announcement of the Parousia in Matt 24:30; but it does not mention the Synoptic title "Human Son" or the "Human One," probably because this christological title was not too familiar in the post-Pauline churches. Matt 24:30 and Rev 1:7 allude to Zech 12:10 ("They shall look on the one whom they have pierced") and share this allusion with John 19:37b. At his eschatological appearance, Christ will appear on the clouds of heaven and manifest openly his sovereignty to the whole world. This return of Christ will mean judgment and calamity to those who have killed him (Rev 19:11ff).

It is interesting to note, however, that, of all the New Testament books, only the Fourth Gospel and Revelation refer to Zech 12:10 and use the verb *exekentēsan*, "they have pierced," which is not found in the LXX. In John 19:37b, the prophecy of Zech 12:10 refers to the incident of the soldier piercing Jesus' side after his death (19:35). The Fourth Gospel explicitly states that this piercing of the side of Jesus was done so "that Scripture might be fulfilled," and it then introduces two scriptural quotations. The second quotation refers to Zech 12:10: "They shall look on him whom they have pierced." The Evangelist has probably taken over this quotation from a source; but he has understood it in the sense of the Hebrew Bible passage, since the mourning of Israel in Zech 12:10-14 is an expression of the "spirit of compassion and supplication" that God pours out on the "inhabitants of Jerusalem" (12:10). Similarly, the writer of the Fourth Gospel understands the scriptural quotation as a salvation prophecy.

Although the prophetic announcement of Christ in Rev 1:7 is a conflation of Zech 12:10 and Dan 7:13, the text of Revelation clearly announces the parousia of Jesus before those who pierced him. Thus it appears that in the Fourth Gospel the citation of Zech 12:10 remains closer to the Hebrew Bible text than that in Revelation. Moreover, the text of Revelation shows greater affinities with the Matthean form of the announcement in the Synoptic apocalypse (Matthew 24; Mark 13; Luke 21). Whether or not the text of Revelation presents the older form of the early Christian apocalyptic text Matt 24:30 is not clear. John's use of the conflation of Hebrew Bible texts in an apocalyptic context, however, suggests that he might have been familiar with an early Christian apocalyptic school or tradition.

The prophetic announcement of the glorious vindication of Christ before the whole world concludes with a vigorous confirmation that combines Greek and Hebrew words in the expression "This is the truth," that is, "Amen." It is God who guarantees that this prophetic announcement will come to pass. Only here and in 21:5 does God speak directly. The first and last letters of the

Greek alphabet characterize God as the "Beginning and the End." The designations: "who is, who was, and who is to come" refer to 1:4 and climax in the title "the Almighty" or, more precisely, "the ruler of the whole world." This frequent title for God in Revelation (4:8; 11:7; 15:3; 16:7, 14; 19:6, 15; 21:22) reflects Revelation's deep theological concern about power. It is God who vouches for the ethos, that is, the trustworthiness and authority, of Revelation's prophetic rhetoric that seeks to effect the pathos of persistent resistance and commitment.

In conclusion, the overall introduction characterizes Revelation both in form and in content as an open prophetic letter. The form of the prophetic letter thus provides the vehicle for the prophetic rhetoric of Revelation's apocalyptic visions, auditions, symbols, and images. The introduction focuses theologically not only on God but also on Christ insofar as it speaks of Christ's revelation to the prophets, Christ's redemptive activity in establishing and loving the community, and the eschatological public manifestation of the Human One before the whole world. Yet it is God, the ruler of the universe, who is the ultimate source and reliable guarantor of the "Revelation of Jesus Christ."

B. Rhetorical Situation in the Cities of Asia Minor
Revelation 1:9—3:22

Introduction

This introductory section allows one to study the careful composition and method of Revelation. After explicitly introducing the author and his situation, the prophetic inaugural vision expands into seven prophetic messages or proclamations. The compositional technique of inclusion ties this section to the entire book, whose main part begins (1:9) and concludes (22:8f) with an emphatic introduction and identification of the author: "I, John." Moreover, the inaugural vision stands framed by the command to write a visionary account and to send it to seven communities in Asia Minor (1:11, 19). Revelation is clearly a literary work, even though it claims as its basis prophetic experience and inspiration.

Careful compositional changes characterize this inaugural vision, which follows closely the outline and content of Daniel 10 but deviates at times in order to express its own prophetic-theological emphasis. Like the vision in Daniel, this inaugural vision in 1:12-19 consists of two parts: a vision ("I saw. . . ," 1:12) and an audition ("He said. . . ," 1:17). The author, however, alters the text of Daniel 10 with features from Daniel 7 (a humanlike figure with a certain kind of hair), from Exodus (robe and girdle), and from Ezekiel (feet and voice). Moreover, he expands the audition with an "I am" saying which is derived from early Christian tradition ("I am the first and the last. . . "). Finally he adds an allegorical interpretation in 1:20.

The so-called seven letters are not actual letters, but they are formalized in such a way that they function as prophetic proclamations to the churches. The introductory formula "thus saith" has in Greek, just as in English, an archaic ring to it. It was used as an introductory formula by the Hebrew prophets (250 times in the LXX). The formula also introduced divine Greek oracles and especially royal edicts of the Persian court as well as of Roman emperors or provincial magistrates. The locution is also found in royal fictional letters. The seven messages are thus best understood as royal edicts or divine oracles in letter form.

Within a carefully composed structure each message follows a rhetorical pattern consisting of the following elements:

1. The command to write;
2. The prophetic-messenger formula (*tade legei*: "thus saith") and the characterization of the speaker, who is Jesus Christ;
3. The following elements and sequence of the "I know" section:
   a. description of situation ("I know that. . . "),
   b. censure ("but I have against you. . . "),
   c. command to repent,
   d. a prophetic-revelatory saying ("look. . . "),
   e. promise of Christ's speedy coming,
   f. exhortation (hold fast);
4. The call to hear is addressed to everyone in the churches and not simply to one particular church;
5. The eschatological promise to those who will overcome addresses again a wider audience and not just the community to whom the message is sent.

The characterizations of Jesus Christ at the beginning of each message repeat features of the inaugural vision and in this way make the messages an integral part of the inaugural vision. Moreover, all the characterizations of Jesus Christ in the beginning, as well as the eschatological promises at the end of the letters, reappear in the final section of the book. In this way, the first and last sections of Revelation stand in close relationship to each other and provide the overall framework for the central section of Revelation. Finally, despite their structural uniformity, the seven prophetic messages are not repetitive or monotonous, but they vary. Four of them contain praise and censure; two communities receive only praise; one is simply censured.

The fact that the author writes in his own name distinguishes him from other apocalyptic writers who often wrote under the auspices of great figures of the past (e.g., Moses, Enoch, Baruch). They did so in order to gain a fictive standpoint from which they could present history in the form of a pronouncement for the future. In contrast, John does not adopt a pseudonym probably because he is not interested either in communicating esoteric knowledge or in predicting schedules for the coming of the end of time. Instead he seeks to provide prophetic interpretation and eschatological exhortation for the Christian communities in Asia Minor to whom he writes. The so-called seven letters therefore appear to occupy structurally the same position that surveys of world history, reviews of heavenly secrets, or the description of heavenly journeys hold in other apocalypses. Since both the messages and the following visions aim at prophetic exhortation, the messages may not be divided from the so-called apocalyptic visions but must be understood as an integral part of the author's overall visionary rhetorical composition.

The so-called seven letters prove that the author is rooted in three Christian prophetic-apocalyptic traditions:

The first tradition. Revelation's roots in the early Christian eschatological tradition come especially to the fore in the exhortation to watch (Ger.: *Weckruf*) and the conqueror's saying (Ger.: *Siegerspruch*) which are repeated in all of the letters to the seven churches of Asia Minor (chaps. 1–3). The exhortation "she/he who has ears, let her/him hear" always has the same form in Greek (*ho echōn ous akousatō*). This form is also found with slight deviations in the Synoptic tradition. The participial form of the messages is similar to that in Matt 11:15 and 13:9, 43, whereas the "if any one" (*ei tis*) form of Rev 13:9 comes closer to Mark 4:23 and 7:16. As the forms of Mark 4:9 or Luke 8:8b and 14:35 indicate, this basic form of the exhortation to watch (*Weckruf*) can be altered. In the Synoptic Gospels it is attached to the parable tradition as well as connected with eschatological discourse. Interestingly, the function of Rev 3:9 in its context is the same as that of Mark 13:14//Matt 24:15c in the Synoptic apocalypse and has a parallel form in Mark 13:18.

The exhortation to watch is also found in *The Gospel of Thomas* (Logia 8, 63, 65, 69). In Logion 21, the two distinct Synoptic traditions—parable-motives and eschatological parenesis—are combined and connected with a *Weckruf*. Since it does not have attestation in pre-Christian literature, it probably originated in the eschatological announcements of early Christian prophecy. This *Sitz im Leben* is suggested also by the fact that the letters of Revelation continue the call to watch (*Weckruf*) with the attestation of the Spirit: "He/she who has an ear let him/her hear what the Spirit says to the churches." The same prophetic understanding is also given elsewhere in the Scriptures (Rev 14:13; 22:17; Acts 13:2; 1 Tim 4:1) as well as in Ignatius, *Letter to the Philadelphians* (7.2). It is to be distinguished from the Paraclete understanding of the Fourth Gospel.

The formal structure of the promise to the victor (*Siegerspruch*) at the end of the seven letters is basically the same, despite variations. The conditional participial clause is followed by the main clause in the future tense (3:21; cf. 2:26). This basic form corresponds to that of the "Sentences of Holy Law" in the Hebrew Bible which were pronounced by early Christian prophets. Outside Revelation, the verb is especially found in 1 John (2:13; 4:4; 5:4-5) and in John 16:33, which belongs with the whole of John 16 to the post-Evangelist, redactional stage. It is therefore often characterized as "Johannine." The promises to the victorious (*Siegersprüche*), however, reflect in content and form more the apocalyptic understanding of *nikaō* ("to conquer"; cf. 4 Ezra 7:127-29: "But if he be victorious, he shall receive"). Whereas Revelation expresses with *ho nikōn* ("the one who conquers") a condition for the future salvation of Christians and uses the past tense of the verb only for Christ (5:5; 3:21), 1 John speaks of Christian victory not as a condition still to be accomplished, but as an act which is already achieved.

The second tradition. Exegetes have long acknowledged that the first seven-fold series of the seals shows remarkable parallelism to the so called Synoptic apocalypse. As we have already seen, the word of Christ in Rev 1:7 is closely related to the announcement of the parousia of the Human One in Matt 24:30. Other allusions include the exhortation to watch (Mark 13:35, 37; Matt 25:13) because Christ or the parousia will come like a thief (Rev 3:2-3; 16:5; cf. Matt 24:42 and Luke 12:39-40. Especially close are Rev 3:3b and Matt 24:50; Luke 12:46). The urgency of the saying and watch and the simile of the thief occur also in the Pauline tradition (1 Thess 5:2-3; 2 Pet 3:10). Paul, however, as distinct from Revelation and the Synoptic passages, specifies that the thief comes "in the night."

The proclamation of the gospel in Rev 14:6 alludes to Mark 13:10 and Matt 24:4, whereas the scene of the eschatological harvest in Rev 14:14-20 refers to Mark 13:26-27 (and parallels) and to the eschatological parable of the Tares (Matt 13:24-43). Interesting references to Luke's form of the apocalyptic discourse are Rev 11:2b (Luke 21:24) as well as the announcement "the time is at hand" (Rev 1:3b; 22:10), which Luke, however, ascribes to those who come in Christ's name and say: "The time is at hand" (Luke 21:8; 13:28). A similar emphasis on the *kairos* as end time and on the nearness of the Lord is found in the Pauline tradition (Rom 13:11; 1 Cor 7:29; Phil 4:5).

The depiction of the beasts in Revelation 13, the Antichrist (13:3, 7b, 8a, 11) and the pseudoprophet (13:11-18; cf. Rev 16:13; 19:20; 20:10), shows affinities with the characterization of the "false christs and prophets" of the apocalyptic discourse in Mark 13:22 (and parallels). In Revelation, as in the Synoptic discourse, we have two related antagonistic figures who deceive the people, if possible even the elect, by doing great signs. A similar tradition is found in 2 Thess 2:3-10 with respect to the "man of lawlessness." Rev 13:11, 13 also shows affinities with the tradition about false prophets in Matt 7:15. A more careful study might show many more affinities to the apocalyptic discourse of the Synoptics, but the above-mentioned texts suffice to indicate that the author was familiar with this early Christian apocalyptic tradition. In view of this familiarity with early Christian apocalyptic it is remarkable that we do not find the Human One (Son of Man) title in Revelation (1:13 and 14:15 have "like" [*homoion*]).

Revelation 3:5c-8 refers to the eschatological Q traditions of Matt 10:32// Luke 12:8 (see also 2 Tim 2:11-12 for the parallel compound "confessing and denying"); Rev 3:21 promises to all Christians what Luke 22:28-30// Matt 19:28 promise to the Twelve; Rev 17:4b recalls Matt 23:25//Luke 11:39; and Rev 18:24 has similarities with Matt 23:35//Luke 11:50. An interesting combination of a saying from the Synoptic apocalypse (Mark 13:29//Matt 24:3) and one from Luke's special material (Luke 12:35-39) is found in the announcement of Rev 3:20, which not only links the expression "the standing of the Lord at the door" with the eschatological feast and table fellowship but, at the same time, allegorizes the parable of Luke. That the expression "standing before the door" is to be understood in an eschatological sense also becomes clear when we compare the saying in Rev 3:20 with Jas 5:9.

The third tradition. An allegorization of the parable tradition can be found in Rev 19:7-8, which describes eschatological salvation using the wedding imagery found in the eschatological parables of Matthew (wedding guest, Matt 22:1-13, and especially Matt 25:1-13). The image of bridegroom and bride is evoked in Mark 2:19 and in John 3:29 it is ascribed to John the Baptist. Both Rev 19:7-8 and the eschatological parables of Matthew place emphasis on the blessing of the wedding guests. Consequently, the marriage imagery in Revelation appears to be closer to Synoptic traditions than to the imagery of Paul. Finally, the author's familiarity not only with Pauline and Synoptic eschatological traditions but also with other forms of early Christian apocalyptic materials is evidenced, for example, by the promise of the "crown of life" in Rev 2:10b, which is also present in Jas 1:12 and 2 Tim 4:8.

In conclusion, the review of traditional materials in chapters 1–3, as well as in Revelation on the whole, has shown that the author uses early Christian prophetic-apocalyptic traditions and understands the words of the book as prophetic *Geistrede* (speech of the Spirit). The author, however, does not *quote* but *uses* various Hebrew Bible and early Christian traditions in order to formulate his own statements. He employs materials that, in content and form, belong to the prophetic-apocalyptic literature of the Hebrew Bible and to early Christian prophetic-apocalyptic traditions. By reappropriating Jewish as well as Christian prophetic traditions, John seeks to establish his own prophetic authority and that of his writing. At the same time, in shaping his own prophetic rhetoric in the literary form of an open letter, he engages in a creative remolding of the prophetic tradition and authority.

Revelation 1:9
The Solidarity of John with His Readers

Revelation 1:9-11 does not simply provide the setting for the introductory "call vision" of the prophet John. It also gives information about the historical-theological setting and the rhetorical situation of the book in general. Like the Hebrew prophets, John locates himself in his own day and age. With the "words of prophecy" he seeks to strengthen the congregations in Asia Minor for a potential clash with the antidivine and dehumanizing powers of their society. Like other early Christian prophets, he claims leadership for the sake of "upbuilding, encouraging, and consoling" (1 Cor 14:3) the community. John derives his authority to do so from his prophetic inspiration rather than from an institutional position. He does not introduce himself with the title of either prophet or teacher but as the "brother and partner" of the audience. He stands in solidarity with them and shares a common experience with those to whom he writes.

The three Greek expressions that characterize the theological and historical situation of John and his readers are very difficult to translate. The first word, *thlipsis*, can mean: agony, distress, ordeal, eschatological tribulation, suffering, oppression. With it, John insists that he shares with Christians in Asia Minor the tribulations of the end time, which consist of possible exile, imprisonment, social ostracism, slander, poverty, economic exploitation, violence, and the constant threat of judicial action. Although scholars debate whether John writes from the island of Patmos because he was there for prophetic inspiration or because of imposed exile, the latter seems more likely in view of the theological emphasis of Revelation. As a result of his prophetic activity and his preaching of Christ, John appears to have already experienced acts of persecution and harassment which in his view also threaten the Christian churches in Asia Minor.

The second term, *basileia*, also may be translated in various ways: kingdom, empire, royal power, kingship, sovereignty, dominion. John, along with the communities, both participates in the eschatological power of God's and Christ's royal reign and shares as a partner in God's empire even in the present. Christians, already appointed in baptism as representative of God's kingdom or empire, however, will exercise their royal power only in the eschatological future. This is the reason why the power of Satan which stands behind the world-empire of Rome will necessarily lead to violent actions against those Christians who are loyal to the empire of God. In Revelation, power confronts power and empire confronts empire. Compromise is not possible.

The third Greek expression, *hypomonē*, can mean: patience, loyal endurance, consistent resistance, steadfastness, perseverance, staying power. Rather than faith or love, *hypomonē* becomes the main Christian virtue in Revelation. According to John, Christian existence is determined by the conjunction of oppressive eschatological tribulations with the Christian claim to share in the divine empire and royal power of God, which requires consistent resistance and steadfast perseverance. This is the challenge facing Christians as representatives of God's power and empire here and now. John's rhetoric insists that he and the audience share the same challenge. This prophetic rhetoric seeks to evoke consistent resistance and commitment as the desired effect upon the audience (*pathos*).

Revelation 1:10-20
The Lord and Judge of the Church

A careful look at the inaugural vision demonstrates why one is justified in calling Revelation a "literary vision." It is impossible to pictorialize or draw this vision, since Revelation is full of image associations which cannot be depicted. Rather, its images and symbols function like words and sentences in a narrative composition. One could say that the author constructs his rhetorical paragraphs and sections with symbols and images rather than with abstract concepts and theological definitions.

Like the prophets of the Hebrew Bible, John introduces his message with a prophetic call-vision. He mentions the island Patmos as the place of this vision and "the Lord's day" (probably Sunday) as the time when the vision took place. John does not claim, however, that he received his prophetic vocation in ecstasy; but he simply uses the classical prophetic formula, "The Spirit came upon me." He also does not say, as popular understanding has it, that he wrote the whole book during or immediately after experiencing the vision.

A comparison of the figure described in Daniel 10 with that of Christ in Revelation 1 indicates that John works in a literary fashion insofar as he utilizes Daniel 10 as his pattern and source text but changes this pattern in several ways. The ways Revelation differs from Daniel 10 indicate what the author wanted to stress or to add. Whereas Dan 10:5 refers to a human being, Revelation refers here and in 14:14 to a humanlike figure, probably in order to allude to the early Christian Son of Man or to the Human One title without explicitly using it in a titular form. This indicates that John is not interested as much in this christological title as he is in the description of the Danielic figure.

The description of the hair (Daniel 7) and of the voice (Ezek 1:25; 43:2) underlines the affinity of Christ to God. Where the humanlike figure in Daniel 10, however, is clothed in linen and girded around the hips, the Christ figure in Revelation is clothed in the long robe of the Jewish high priest (Ezek 9:2; Exod 28:4, 31) and girded around the chest (Ezek 44:18). These specific changes to the Daniel text seem to stress Christ's royal/priestly character. Since in New Testament times the role of the high priest entailed not just cultic but also kingly functions and honors, these changes underline both the royal and the cultic functions of the "One in Human Likeness."

The symbol of the two-edged sword identifies Christ as judge of the communities (see also Rev 2:16) and designates him in Rev 19:15 as judge of the nations. Thus, the first and last sections of Revelation open with the image of Christ as the eschatological judge. The author of Revelation not only threatens the nations with judgment but also places the Christian community under the judgment of Christ. In doing so, he discourages his readers/hearers from projecting evil and failure only onto others without acknowledging their own accountability for their actions. At the same time, he assures them that Christ not only has conquered death but that he, as the Living One, also has control over the destructive powers of death.

The inaugural vision's main theological interest, therefore, lies in the present relationship of Christ to the Christian community. John underlines this interest in 1:20 by explicitly singling out two features of the inaugural vision for interpretation: the vision (1) of Christ standing in the midst of seven golden lamp stands and (2) of Christ holding seven stars in his right hand. The seven-branched candelabra reminds one of the golden temple menorah which was a symbol of the Jewish people in the first century. Rev 1:20 identifies this candelabra with the Christian community to whom the book is addressed. The images of 1:12f and 2:1 thus evoke the theological promise expressed in Lev 26:12: "I will walk among you, and will be your God, and you shall be my people." This theological promise that is here expressed symbolically will become fully realized in the eschatological future, when God will live among the people of God (Rev 21:3).

The image of the seven stars in the right hand of Christ is more difficult to understand since we do not find it in the Hebrew Bible. The seven stars may refer to the seven planets that symbolized the universal dominion of the Roman emperor. If this is the case, this image depicts Christ as analogous to the Roman emperor as being the universal ruler of the world; however, the explication given in 1:20 appears to prohibit such an interpretation of the seven stars because it explicitly identifies the seven stars with the angels of the churches receiving the prophetic messages.

The identity of the seven angels has long puzzled exegetes. Since Revelation does not mention bishops anywhere else, it is unlikely that bishops are addressed here as some exegetes have suggested. Insofar as angels in Revelation are usually heavenly beings and communicators, the seven angels more likely represent the patron angels of the churches. The close relationship of the functions of angel and prophet in Revelation (19:10; 22:9) indicates that the angels could also stand for the prophetic communication of the leadership in the communities. The following reasons support this last hypothesis: First, John seems to be the head of a prophetic school or circle (22:9). Second, at the conclusion of the individual messages it is the Spirit who speaks to the communities. In light of these, the interpretation of the seven stars in 1:20 may seek to focus Christ's universal power on his relationship to the Christian communities. Christ exercises authority over them through prophetic communication announcing the eschatological promises and warnings of the Spirit.

Revelation 2:1—3:22
Prophetic Censure and Encouragement

The so-called "seven letters" are not real letters. Rather, they function as messages that all follow the same rhetorical pattern. They form a unit which is an integral part of Revelation's inaugural vision. As prophetic messages, they address the whole church in Asia Minor. The number seven symbolically indicates their universal character. Geographically, all seven communities mentioned are situated on main Roman roads and form a circuit starting from Ephesus, the nearest city to Patmos. They thus symbolically represent the whole church in Asia Minor, one of the main centers of early Christianity.

Since the messages are not just addressed to individual communities but were designed to be read by all of them, it seems best not to discuss them separately but to attempt a cumulative analysis. They together perform the rhetorical function of characterizing the rhetorical setting of the book as a whole. Thus the seven messages give a schematized picture of the ecclesial situation in Asia Minor. Revelation elaborates this rhetorical situation by pointing to the strengths and weaknesses of the communities.

The exhortations of the seven-message section aim primarily at prophetic interpretation and critical evaluation. The strength of the Christian community in Asia Minor consists: in mutual love, in service to others, in fidelity and steadfastness, in the keeping of God's word and the rejecting of false teachers, in the confession of its faith even during persecution, and in consistent resistance. The author emphasizes the works, or the *praxis*, of the Asian churches. However, not all the churches are still doing "the works of their first love." Some have not rejected the false teachers; some are no longer "alive"; and some of them are "tepid" and in danger of being cast away. John enjoins them to "remember" what Christ did for them, to repent, to change radically their orientation and commitment, to resist faithfully, and to endure under all conditions.

How does the author counteract the political situation and theological issue debated in the seven churches? Revelation indicates that some of them have already experienced discrimination and harassment from their Jewish co-religionists and particularly from their Asian-Roman neighbors and the provincial authorities. Two major developments which occurred under the Flavian emperors Vespasian (69–79), Titus (79–81), and Domitian (81–96) complicated their precarious position, both socially and religiously.

The first development. Under the Flavians, especially Domitian, the Asian provinces strongly promoted the imperial cult. Domitian is said to have demanded that the populace acclaim him as "Lord and God" and participate in emperor worship. Even if he did not introduce this title, such participation in the imperial cult as the religion of the state was generally regarded as a sign of political loyalty since the emperor was seen as the living head of the state and the guardian of its fortunes.

The majority of the cities to which the prophetic messages are addressed were dedicated to the promotion of this Roman civil religion. Ephesus, the greatest city of the Roman province Asia, was the seat of the proconsul and competed with Pergamum for the recognition of its primacy. Like Smyrna it was a center of the imperial cult and famous for its gladiatorial games. Pergamum, a citadel of Hellenistic civilization in Asia, claimed to be the official center of the imperial cult. Already, in 29 B.C.E., the city had received permission to build a temple to the "divine Augustus and the goddess Roma." Revelation's reference to the "throne of Satan" might be an allusion to this temple. In Thyatira, the emperor was worshiped also as Apollo incarnate and as the son of Zeus. In 26 C.E., Sardis competed with ten other Asian cities for the right to build a temple in honor of the emperor, but lost out to Smyrna. Laodicea was known not only as the wealthiest city of Phrygia but also as a center of the imperial cult.

In such an environment, Christians were bound to experience increasing conflicts with the official provincial civil religion, since they acclaimed Jesus Christ and not the emperor as their Lord and God. Although we cannot document a full-fledged, legally sanctioned persecution of Christians before the second century, Revelation and other New Testament writings know of persecution and harassment. James, the brother of Jesus, and also Steven were stoned to death. Peter and Paul were executed in the 60s. Under Nero, Christians of Rome were condemned to death in 64 C.E. John himself may have experienced political exile and he knew that individual Christians were harassed, persecuted, and killed (e.g., Antipas). John's rhetoric anticipates an increase of harassments and difficulties in the near future. His experience of and anticipation of persecution constitutes the rhetorical situation inscribed in the text.

The second development. The situation of Christians in Asia Minor was aggravated because Jewish Christians like John were less and less able to claim their political privileges and identity as Jews. The Jewish people had received the privilege of practicing their religion in any part of the Roman Empire, but they were exempted from obligations of military service as well as giving obeisance to the Roman religion. Under the Flavians, however, the situation of the Jewish people became more precarious. Vespasian ordered that all Jews and proselytes now had to pay a special tax to the Romans in place of the tax formerly paid to the Jerusalem temple. Domitian enforced the tax and exacted its payment especially from proselytes and God-fearers who were not Jews by birth. In addition, the destruction of Jerusalem and the temple compelled the Jewish community to draw its religious and ethnic boundaries more clearly. If Jews were excluded from the synagogue because they were confessing Christians, such Jews could no longer claim the protection granted by Roman law to Judaism.

The messages to Smyrna and Philadelphia seem to reflect such a conflict. John's identification of the synagogue as a congregation of Satan should not be misread as anti-Semitism since the author expresses great appreciation for true Judaism. As a Jew, John must have been aware that established Jewish communities could not afford to tolerate any anti-Roman deviance that jeopardized their political status. The Christian Jews of Philadelphia who ran into difficulties with the local synagogue seem to have been poor and powerless. They receive assurance that Christ as the Davidic Messiah will keep open for them the "door" to the eschatological future and guarantee their citizenship in the New Jerusalem.

Everyday experiences of harassment, persecution, and hostility from pagan as well as Jewish neighbors and from the provincial authorities must have challenged the community's faith in Christ as "Lord and King" of the world. Like John, Christians in Asia Minor must have realized again and again that their actual experience and political situation in no way supported their theological and christological convictions of God's supreme power. Such a tension and contradiction between everyday experience of tribulation and the theological conviction to share in God's royal power must have provoked difficult theological questions: Why do Christians have to suffer if Christ is the true ruler of the world? Why are Christians persecuted if the living God is on their side and the gods of the other religions are powerless idols? Why did Christ not return in glory to prevent the further sufferings of his followers and communities? These pressing theological questions seem to have been answered differently by various leading prophets in the churches of Asia Minor. Revelation implicitly informs us of this theological debate by arguing against rival Christian apostles and prophets who seem to have had greater influence than John within several of the communities in Asia Minor.

John explicitly polemicizes against these rival Christian prophets in the messages addressed to the churches in Ephesus, Pergamum, and Thyatira. Ephesus earns praise because it has rejected the false prophets and shown hatred for the works of the so-called Nicolaitans, whereas Pergamum receives criticism for tolerating those who hold to the teachings of Balaam. The community in Thyatira, in turn, provokes censure because it has accepted the influence and teaching of a woman prophet and her school. All three terms—Nicolaitans, Balaam, and Jezebel—theologically label probably the same group of Christian prophets who allowed their followers to eat food that had been sacrificed to idols and to participate in pagan religious festivities. This theological stance probably offered political, economic, and professional advantages to Christians living in the prosperous trading cities of Asia Minor, since the meat sacrificed to idols was served at meetings of trade guilds and business associations as well as at private receptions. It provided an alternative theological perspective to the "either/or" rhetoric of John because it proposed a theological compromise. This alternative prophetic rhetoric allowed Christian believers to participate actively in the commercial, political, and social life of their cities and the Empire.

How might this prophetic group have argued theologically for such an integration into pagan society? As Jewish Christians in Corinth had done some forty years earlier, they might have reasoned that "idols are nothing" (1 Cor 8:4) and that therefore Christians could eat food previously sacrificed to idols. Since Christians knew, as did most educated Romans or Asians, that Caesar's claim to divinity was nothing more than a constitutional fiction for promoting political loyalty to Rome, there was no need for refusing to pay honor to the emperor. Did not the great apostle Paul who had founded some of the Asian communities demand that one submit to the authorities of the state because they were ordained by God (Rom 13:1-7)? That Christians at the end of the first century did argue in such a fashion is evident from the First Epistle of Peter, which admonishes persecuted Christians to "honor the emperor" (2:17). Since participation in the imperial cult did not require creedal adherence, it was possible to honor the emperor without compromising one's faith in Jesus Christ.

Moreover, this alternative prophetic rhetoric might have argued that to oppose the imperial cult and to refuse participation in societal-religious affairs would mean taking too seriously the sovereignty claims of the emperor and the reality of idols. The political claims of the emperor and state on the one hand, and the religious claims of God and Christ on the other hand, do not conflict with each other because both types of claims belong to radically different orders (John 18:36-38). Jesus Christ's claim to kingship and power, they might have reasoned, is not of a political nature. Rather, it affects solely the spiritual life of Christians and the religious dimensions of the church. Christians are liberated from this world; and by virtue of their baptism, they share already in the royal power and glory of the Enthroned. No one, not even Satan, can harm the elect, for they possess insight into the very depths of the demonic and the divine. If this is the case, they might have asked, why go to prison for a cause not worth dying for? Is it not true that idols have no real existence, and what else is the imperial image but an idol? To say otherwise would be bad theology or religious fanaticism.

In responding to this theological challenge, John, like Paul before him, stresses that behind idols stands the demonic power of Satan, the ultimate adversary of God and of Christians. No compromise can be made between one's loyalty to God and one's loyalty to Caesar because God and Christ are the true rulers of the world and the nations. This theological response of John appears to be rooted in a different sociopolitical experience and view of the world. John may have been exiled and persecuted because of his witness to Jesus, but the two communities that receive Christ's praise and not his censure appear to have been poor and without power. In contrast, those communities receiving only censure are in John's judgment rich and complacent.

It seems, therefore, that John advocates an uncompromising theological stance because he and his followers view the dehumanizing powers of Rome and its allies as theologically so destructive and oppressive that a compromise with them would mean a denial of God's life-giving and saving power. The visionary rhetoric of the inaugural vision insists, therefore, that Christ is alive, although he was killed. Those who resist the powers of death that threaten to destroy their lives now will, in the future, share in the royal power of God and Jesus Christ. To those who are poor and exploited now, the "promises to the victor" guarantee the essentials of life for the eschatological future: food, clothing, home, citizenship, security, honor, power. These promises are made not to the rich, the satisfied, and the influential but to those who are poor, persecuted, and suffering in the communities of Asia Minor in order to encourage them to consistent resistance and faithful commitment.

C. Opening the Sealed Scroll:
Exodus Plagues
Revelation 4:1—9:21

Introduction

The opening remark in 4:1 links the visions of chapters 4–5 to the preceding seven series of the prophetic messages by identifying the speaker (the first trumpet voice) with the one introducing the inaugural vision in 1:10, 12 (a voice like a trumpet). Moreover, the last eschatological promise to the victors (3:21f) concluding the seven-letter series not only points to the image of the throne, the central symbol in the New Jerusalem vision, but it also points to chapters 4–5, which picture the throne of God and envision the victorious Christ receiving his share of God's ruling power. By taking possession of the sevenfold sealed scroll, the Lamb is enthroned as the eschatological Lord of the world who executes the three series of plague septets in order to liberate the new-Exodus people of God. The opening of the seals sets off seven cycles of eschatological trumpets (8:2—9:21; 11:15-19), whose plagues are intensified in turn by the final seven cycle of the bowl septet (15:1, 5—16:21). All three seven-series of plagues speak about the same eschatological events and elaborate the traditional characteristics of the end time in visionary form. The seven sequences of plagues are therefore patterned after a thematic-theological scheme and a temporal-chronological one.

Revelation 4:1—5:14
God, the Creator, and Christ, the Liberator

Although the seven visions of seals are structurally integrated with chapters 4–5 and should be read together with the introductory vision as a literary unit, I am separating them here from the introductory vision for pragmatic reasons. This procedure is justified insofar as chapters 4–5 provide not only the setting for the breaking of the seals but also the basis for the understanding of the whole book. Their central image is political. The throne image (Rev 4:2-6, 9-10; 5:1, 6-7, 11, 13), occurs again and again like a keynote symbol throughout the whole book (Rev 1:4; 2:13; 3:21; 6:16; 7:9-11, 15, 17; 8:3; 11:16; 12:5; 13:2; 14:3; 16:10, 17; 19:4-5; 20:4, 11-12; 21:5; 22:1, 3). In this way, chapters 4–5 lay the rhetorical foundation and provide the key symbolic images for all that follows.

The central theological question of chapters 4–5 as well as of the whole book is: Who is the true Lord of this world? This theological question of power is addressed and elaborated with the cosmological imagery and symbolic language of chapters 4–5—derived from Hebrew-Jewish, Hellenistic, and Roman royal tradition and imagery—because Christ has been victorious and he shares in the throne and power of God. Enthroned in eternal majesty and power, the victorious Christ, with God, exercises true lordship over the world. In the visionary language of symbol and myth, chapters 4–5 develop the concluding statement of 3:21: "To those victorious I will grant a place on my throne, as I myself was victorious and share the throne of my Father."

While the first seven-cycle of the prophetic message-series interprets the actual situation of the Asian churches here on earth from the perspective of the resurrected Christ, chapters 4–5 describe the heavenly reality of divine power from the perspective of the seer. John claims in a prophetic revelation to have received a glimpse of the world of God and now seeks to communicate it in royal language and mythological imagery. John's artistic-rhetorical competence shows itself in his ability to integrate different features of Isa 6:1ff; Ezek 1:26-28; Dan 7:9; 1 Kgs 22:19; 1 Enoch 39f; and 2 Enoch 20–22 into an overall picture of great magnificence. Instead of attempting to explain every feature of this glorious vision in detail, one must primarily acquire an overall impression of the whole composition of the vision in order to do justice to its powerful rhetoric.

John describes heaven not so much as a temple but as an oriental or Roman sovereign's throne hall. God reigns like an Oriental or Hellenistic ruler in the splendor of unapproachable light surrounded by the highest beings of the celestial court. The polished pavement of the royal hall stretches out before the throne like a sea of crystal-clear glass mirroring the resplendent majesty of the One on the throne. Lightning, thunder, and voices—the traditional signs of theophany—emanate from the throne. Burning before the throne are seven lamps of fire, which are interpreted to be the symbols of the divine Spirit. As befits the "King of Kings," twenty-four angelic vassals, seated on thrones and wearing crowns of gold, as well as four living creatures, the representatives of all of creation, attend to the One on the throne. Although exegetes widely disagree about the identity of the twenty-four elders and the four living beings, it seems clear that the author understands them as attendants of the royal court who give homage and praise to the all-powerful ruler of the universe.

The central figure of the whole vision is clearly God enthroned in great splendor and surrounded by a court of angelic principalities and powers. Just as the Roman emperor was depicted as surrounded by his friends and advisers when dispensing justice, so is God here seen in the role of judge. Just as the Roman emperor surrounded by the court was depicted as holding a *libellus*, a petition or letter in the form of an open scroll, so God is seen as holding a *biblion*, a scroll with seven seals. No attempt, however, is made to visualize God in human form. The glorious presence of the "One on the throne" manifests itself in the brilliance of light reflected by the precious stones of opaque diamondlike jasper, blood-red sardis, and colorless emerald refracting a rainbow of prismatic colors, the sign of God's covenant with creation. The whole vision climaxes in the hymnic acclamation of the almighty Creator. The thrice-holy and worthy acclamation in vv. 8-11 expresses and emphasizes the glory and power of the almighty Creator whose eschatological manifestation on earth is near.

The presentation of golden crowns before the emperor (*proskynēsis*) is part of the court ceremony taken over from Hellenistic-Oriental kingship rituals. According to the Roman writer Tacitus, the Parthian king Tiridates placed his diadem before the image of Nero in order to give homage to the Roman emperor. Here in Revelation, too, the twenty-four angelic vassal-kings cast their crowns before the One on the throne, acknowledging the almighty Creator with the political-symbolic language of the day. Even Domitian is said to have been acclaimed as "Lord and God." Moreover, the acclamation "worthy are you" greeted the triumphal entrance of the emperor. Like the Roman emperor, God, the Creator and all-powerful Regent of this world, receives in this vision unceasing honor and homage.

The grandiose vision of God in chapter 4 sets the stage for the symbolic vision of Christ in chapter 5. The whole chapter appears to be a well-composed literary unit consisting of concentric segments. After the description of the sealed scroll (v. 1), the question of the angel searching for the one worthy to open the seals follows (v. 2). The importance of this quest is underscored in three ways: through the silence of the cosmos (v. 3), through the weeping of the seer (v. 4), and through the consolation by the elder who points to the one who is worthy (v. 5). After the Lamb is announced to the heavenly court, the Lamb appears and takes the scroll from the outstretched hand of the One on the throne (vv. 6-7).

As the description of the scene in chapter 5 gradually expands to its climax, so also the conclusion of the heavenly praise proceeds in four steps: (1) The "new song" (vv. 9-10) corresponds to the consolation by the elder (v. 5); (2) the hymn of the angels (vv. 11-12) corresponds to the weeping of the seer (v. 4); (3) the praise of the world (v. 13) seems to be the counterpart to the silence of the cosmos (v. 3); and (4) the affirmative Amen of the four living creatures and the adoration of the elders (v. 14) answers the question of the angel (v. 2). As in chapter 4, so chapter 5 climaxes in the hymnic homage of the heavenly court.

The central figure of the composition is the lionlike Lamb, an image which occurs twenty-eight times in Revelation and always appears to signify the resurrected Christ. Although the reasons why the author employs this image for Christ remain unclear, his diction and imagery are quite different from those of the Fourth Gospel. With this image, Revelation seems either to invoke the notion of the paschal lamb, to refer to the sacrificial lambs of the temple, or to allude to the astrological sign of Aries. In any case, the vision characterizes the Lamb as the victor who had to suffer death but is alive again.

That the author does not think in realistic pictures but, rather, formulates his theology in the form of a literary vision becomes obvious when he identifies the figure of the Lamb as the "lion of the tribe of Judah" and as the "root of David." Both images designate Christ as the fulfillment of all Jewish messianic hopes. The "seven horns" and the "seven eyes," identified as the seven spirits sent out into all the earth, signify the fullness of power and omniscient control over the world. The Lamb, therefore, is the only one in the whole universe who stands worthy to receive and to open the sevenfold sealed book or scroll.

The enigmatic symbol of the sevenfold sealed scroll has received many different interpretations; however, it seems best to derive its meaning from its compositional context. According to ancient Oriental mythology, the highest God possesses books or plates in which the destiny of the world is inscribed.

In the ritual enthronement of the Great King, these books are given to the king as a sign that he now has power over the world. This power entails the rendering of judgment and the execution of justice as the primary role of the emperor. If this contextualization is correct, the author appears to picture the enthronement of Jesus Christ as ruler and judge of the world and of its destiny by stressing that only the Lamb is worthy to receive the sealed scroll and to open its seals. Rev 5:12 confirms such an interpretation of this visionary rhetoric insofar as the hymn explicitly states that the Lamb's "taking over" or "receiving" of the sevenfold sealed scroll means receiving power and honor. By opening the seals, Christ exercises this power, setting in motion the events of the end time. Hence Christians can recognize, even in the execution of the eschatological plagues over the world, the power and dominion of their Lord.

The "new song" in 5:9-10 underlines three reasons why the Lamb is worthy to assume the eschatological reign over the world:

First: The Lamb proves worthy because it has suffered a violent death. The verb "slain" probably alludes to the slaughtering of the paschal lamb, an image used early in the Christian tradition to interpret Jesus' execution (1 Cor 5:7; 1 Pet 1:18). This image evokes the memory of Israel's exodus and liberation, which in Judaism served as a prototype for the final eschatological salvation.

Second: The Lamb's worthiness derives from its activity as God's agent who traveled throughout the world to purchase the freedom of people from all nations. This metaphoric language most probably refers to the ransom of prisoners of war who were deported to the countries of the victors and could be ransomed by a purchasing agent of their own home country. The image also alludes to the Exodus tradition. As the blood of the paschal lamb signified the liberation of Israel from the bondage of Egypt, so has the death of Christ made possible the liberation of Christians from their universal bondage.

Third: The final reason which the hymn gives for the Lamb's worthiness focuses on the positive goal of Christ's redemptive activity. According to Roman law, those prisoners of war who were ransomed were brought back home and reintegrated into their own nation. In the same way, those who were ransomed by Christ for God were liberated in order to constitute here and now a "kingdom of priests" (1:6); however, John stresses here that they are to exercise their royal power only in the eschatological future on earth. Just as the Exodus led to the constitution of Israel as a special empire and priestly nation for Yahweh (Exod 19:6), so has Christ created the community of the redeemed as the nation or empire on earth that acknowledges and witnesses to the power and reign of God and Christ already in the midst of "tribulation." As the empire constituted for God, the redeemed are the anti-empire to the Roman Empire. The author, however, is careful to assert that only those

Christians who, like Christ, are victorious will exercise royal power in the eschatological future.

In summary, the new song of the heavenly court expresses redemption and salvation in economic language and political imagery. It understands it as an event analogous to the liberation of Israel from the slavery of Egypt. Insofar as John utilizes sociopolitical language in 5:9-10, he transforms the anthropological understanding of redemption expressed in the traditional baptismal formula of 1:5-6 into a sociopolitical one. Just as the exodus of Israel resulted in the election of Israel as a special nation and kingdom for Yahweh, so does the redemption of the Lamb's followers who were elected from the nations constitute a new alternative kingdom or empire whose members are priests. Seeking to prevent the spiritualist illusion that Christians exercise their royal power already in the present, John adds the corrective promise that those who are redeemed through Christ's death will reign on earth in the eschatological future (20:4-6). Final redemption from the oppressive power of the nations and the Satanic empire is only possible when God and Christ reign on a "new earth" where death no longer exists (21:4). In short, John's prophetic rhetoric insists that final redemption and salvation does not just pertain to the individual soul but require that the entire world be free of suffering and oppression.

Revelation 6:1-17
The Great Tribulation of the End Time

Structurally, the series of seven seals is clearly linked to chapter 5 and grouped. The first four seal visions parallel each other insofar as they follow the same narrative pattern: After a command from the four living creatures, the release of a rider and a horse occurs. The conclusion of this pattern stresses the destructive powers of the rider whereas the different colors of the horses point to the different functions of the riders. The attribute characterizing each rider in turn elaborates this function symbolically. In contrast to the first four seal visions, the fifth and sixth seal visions receive a different and more elaborate structuring that indicates their significance for the overall composition. The twofold interlude preceding the opening of the last seal is very short and enigmatic. Formally, the opening of the seals gradually prepares us for the revelation of the scroll's contents. The scroll is open only when all the seven seals have been removed. The whole series contains many allusions to texts of the Hebrew Bible but does not follow a pattern derived from the Hebrew Bible or other texts familiar to us. The whole literary vision-series appears then to be the creative work of the author.

Obviously, the second, third, and fourth seal visions symbolize the destructive powers of internal strife and civil war, inflation, and famine that devastate especially the poor. These visions also portray the destructive powers of pestilence and death as the sum of all oppressive powers. Although the overall rhetorical intention of the first four seal visions is clear, the meaning of the first seal remains debatable. Because 19:11ff describes the parousia-Christ in a similar fashion to the first seal vision, some scholars suggest that the first rider is the victorious Christ who sets the sequence of the seal-events in motion. Pointing to Mark 13:10, others identify the first rider as the hypostatized figure of the Gospel conquering the whole world. Yet, the meaning-context of the other six seals appears to point to a different interpretation. The repeated assertion that divine permission was granted for unleashing the plagues speaks against such a theological or christological interpretation of the first rider.

John clearly pictures this first rider as a victorious military commander in chief riding in a triumphal procession. The bow, the sign of military prowess, alludes to its use not only by Parthians but also by Babylonians. John's audience would have immediately grasped that the first rider with the bow refers to the Parthians since they were famous as mounted archers. The image of the royal, conquering, mounted archer evokes the memory of the Parthian victory over the Romans, who were defeated three times (in 53 B.C.E., 35 B.C.E., and 62 C.E.) by the Parthian cavalry. Moreover, according to Jer 51:56, Babylon's warriors were taken captive and their bows were broken. In the symbolic discourse of Revelation, the rider with the bow reveals that the expansionistic military power of Babylon/Rome will be overcome. If that is the case, the first rider functions as the precursor of the victorious parousia-Christ.

The first four seals then do not portray a sequence of events but instead reveal and highlight the true nature of Roman power and rule. They describe: the defeat of the expansionist military rule of the Roman Empire; the inner strife and war undermining Rome's claim to worldwide peace wrought by Augustus (Pax Romana); the concomitant inflation that deprived especially the poor of their essential food sustenance; and last but not least, pestilence and death as bitter consequences of imperialistic war, civil strife, and epidemics of hunger. In sum, the first four riders function to articulate symbolically a sociopolitical critique of imperial rule. They identify this rule as the cause of all the sufferings characteristic of the end time which has been inaugurated with the death and resurrection of Christ. Although the seven seal plagues are set in motion by the Lamb as the agent who opens the seals, John does not assert that these calamities are decreed by God. God authorizes the calamities but does not will them. Rather, Revelation's visionary rhetoric reveals the true nature of the reality and power of Babylon/Rome in its inevitable collapse. The repeated passive-apocalyptic expression—"it was given"—communicates John's theological conviction that these calamities do not happen without the knowledge and authorization of God.

The fifth seal (6:9-11) uses sacrificial terms for characterizing those who were slaughtered and killed because of their witness to God and Christ. The slaughtered ask the enduring question of the vanquished who suffer unbearable injustice and oppression: How long, O Lord? They ask the centuries-old question of those who suffer for God's cause and justice: When, O God, will you vindicate our faith in you and restore justice in the face of those who oppress and persecute us throughout the world? This is not only a plea for the vindication of those who are oppressed and slaughtered, but it is also a plea for the vindication of God in the eyes of those who have placed their trust in God.

Exegetes, who generally do not suffer unbearable oppression and are not tormented by God's apparent toleration of injustice, tend to label this outcry for justice as unchristian and contrary to the preaching of the gospel. One can adjudicate the central quest of Revelation in theological terms, however, only if one comprehends the anguish that fuels this outcry for justice and vindication, for divine revenge and restitution for so many lives taken, and for so much blood unnecessarily shed.

In calling God "sovereign," John appears to allude to the fact that those who suffer injustice and have been killed acknowledge God and not the emperor as their true sovereign. Similarly, the Jewish historian Josephus reports that like the souls crying out for justice, the Zealots endured torture and execution rather than acknowledge the Roman emperor as sovereign. Those slain receive white robes, probably as a sign that they will participate in the marriage feast of the Lamb (19:8). At the same time they learn that they will have to wait only a short time until the numbers of those who still must suffer death will be complete. The length of this short time and the day of justice depends not only on God but also on those Christians still living with their decision for martyrdom. The visionary rhetoric of the author clearly seeks to instill an ethic of resistance by linking the staying power and commitment of his audience to the length of the end-time tribulations.

The death and suffering of the slaughtered will be vindicated only in the final judgment, and only then will the injustice of the present political world-power be avenged. While Rev 6:9-11 articulates the outcry of the slaughtered for justice and retribution and 16:5-7 and 18:20 confirm that this outcry has been heard and responded to, 20:4-6 stresses the positive result of the judgment of God for those killed: They will take part in the first resurrection and actively participate in the messianic reign. Thus, the vision of 6:9-11 has a key rhetorical position within the overall narrative of Revelation.

The opening of the seals reaches its climax with the sixth seal describing the "Day of the Lord" in terms of vast catastrophes and natural cataclysms. The portents in the heavens are so terrible that they can only be understood in apocalyptic terms to mean the final dissolution of the whole world. The language and imagery of this seal vision is hyperbolic rather than descriptive or predictive of actual events. Such an apocalyptic rhetoric of cosmic cataclysm impresses on the audience how terrible the anger and wrath of God and of the Lamb will be. While the first four seals link the present sociopolitical troubles of the audience with the destructive powers of the eschatological time of tribulation, the sixth seal rhetorically portrays the judgment and punishment of the kings and powerful leaders of the earth with the generals and the rich encountering the wrath of the One on the throne. Thus, this seal is quite different from the preceding ones that describe in apocalyptic language and imagery the political, economic, and religious oppression characterizing the end time.

Early Christian apocalyptic beliefs and concepts clearly determine the literary pattern of the seven seals. Early Christians believed themselves to live in the "last days." The death and resurrection of Christ had already inaugurated the eschatological end time. It was the exalted and crucified Christ who broke the seals and set the end-time events in motion. The Synoptic apocalypse (Mark 13 and its parallels) envisions that these end-time events will unfold in two periods or stages of development. After the "great tribulation" has passed, the Christ will return in glory and the "Day of the Lord" will come. Inaugurating and accompanying these events will be earthquakes, portents in heaven, cosmic cataclysms, and the final dissolution of the world.

Not only wars, insurrections, famines, and pestilence, but also the persecution of the elect and the appearance of false prophets, false Christs who can do miraculous deeds as well as preach the Gospel, will determine the short time before the cataclysmic cosmic end-time events as a time of suffering and tribulation. The first five seals appear to allude to most of these upheavals and events. The experience of suffering and oppression is a sign that Christians are living in the last days. God will shortly bring about the cosmic-cataclysmic events to vindicate the suffering of the righteous and to punish all oppressive, dehumanizing powers. This distinction of the two periods of the end time becomes crucial for understanding that the seal septet has a function different from that of the bowl visions and the trumpet visions.

Revelation 7 : 1—8 : 1
The Eschatological Protection
and Salvation of the Elect

In structure and content, chapter 7 interrupts the seal septet insofar as it delays the opening of the last seal and keeps the reader in suspense. This interlude does not speak of the sufferings of the end time but appears to disclose the divine protection and salvation of those "who stand firm to the end" (Mark 13:13). The two visionary sections of chapter 7 are best understood when related to the two periods of the end time pictured in symbolic fashion through the opening of the preceding six seal visions. The vision in Rev 7:1-8 seems to provide an answer to the concluding question of the sixth seal vision: Who can be saved from the wrath and cosmic cataclysms of the "Lord's Day?" (6:17). Rev 7:9-17 in turn pictures those who have "come out of the great tribulation" (7:14). It is the same tribulation which the opening of the first five seals has visualized.

From a compositional point of view, it is significant that the vision and audition of 7:9-12 receives an explicit and extensive interpretation in 7:13-17, paralleled only by the long explanation in 17:7-18 regarding Babylon the Great, drunk with the blood of the saints (17:1-6). In short, the content of the vision in 7:1-8 appears to respond to the question of who can survive the wrath of God and the Lamb, whereas the second vision and its interpretation point to those who have "endured to the end" and therefore participate in eschatological salvation.

The first vision (Rev 7:1-8). In the Hebrew Bible and in Jewish apocalyptic literature, the four winds act as destructive agents of God. For instance, according to Jer 49:36, the four winds carry out Yahweh's verdict against Elam. In Dan 7:2, the four winds send forth the four terrible beasts on their destructive mission. Similarly, in Revelation 7, the four winds also are destructive powers. Yet their action is delayed until God's servants are sealed.

The sealing action with its many possible meanings and its complexities of allusion evokes a rich imagery of symbols. The symbolic action of sealing could allude either to the names of the twelve tribes engraved on the breastplate of the Jewish high priest, to the Jewish custom of wearing phylacteries, to the branding of a slave with a mark, to Christian baptism, to the protective mark of Ezekiel 9, to the blood-mark of the Exodus lamb, to the oriental custom of marking one's belongings with the seal of one's ring, or to all of the above. Rev 9:4 supports the interpretation of the sealing as a sign of protection during the cataclysmic events of the cosmic plagues. The eschatological plagues will kill only those who do not have the seal of God.

Some scholars argue that the sealing cannot have the effect of protecting Christians from suffering, for the author's rhetoric calls Christians to endure sufferings and death. Such an objection, however, overlooks the fact that the symbolic sealing action does not protect anyone from the sufferings of the great tribulation caused by the evil powers presented in the first five seals. Rather, it offers protection from the final wrath of God and of the Lamb. Christians are marked so that they may remain safe in the final eschatological cataclysms. The function of sealing could be compared to the marking of the door of the house with the blood of the paschal lamb designed to protect the Israelites from the Exodus plagues, which initiated the liberation of Israel. The symbolic act of sealing could also derive from Ezek 9:4-6, where God commanded an angel to mark those citizens of Jerusalem who rejected the city's abominations. Those marked would be protected during the judgment of the city.

A great deal has been written about the identity of the 144,000 members of the tribes of Israel who were sealed. It is clear, however, that they are a figure contrasted with the great multitude in 7:9 who are coming from all nations. In contrast with the multitude that cannot be counted, the figure 144,000 represents an immense but definite number; therefore, some argue that the limited number 144,000 refers to the martyrs who will be saved. The vision of the 144,000, however, seems to refer to people on earth (7:1, 3) and not to the eschatological bliss of the elect. Another interpretation suggests that the 144,000 represent Jewish Christians who have remained faithful as distinguished from the great multitude symbolizing gentile Christians. However, the vision of sealing appears not to refer to eschatological salvation but to divine protection during the turmoil of the Last Day. It is, therefore, unlikely that only Jewish Christians would experience such protection. Moreover, the twelve tribes of Israel were no longer a historical but only a theological entity, since in John's time only two tribes were still in existence.

Because the restitution of the twelve tribes of Israel was expected to happen in the eschatological end time (Ezekiel 47–48), this vision of the 144,000 may allude to the early Christian tradition that believed the church to be the restored "Israel of God" (Gal 6:16). The Epistle of James, written to Christians scattered in the Roman Empire, for instance, addresses them as the "twelve tribes in the dispersion." The author of Revelation might utilize Jewish traditions in order to express the conviction that the fate of those Christians experiencing God's judgment day is "sealed" for salvation. Like 1 Peter 2, Revelation applies Exod 19:5-6 to the Christian community and thereby stresses its continuity with Israel as the elect "people of God." It is thus likely that in Rev 7:1-7 the twelve tribes signify the eschatologically restored Israel of which the church is a significant part. The limited number 144,000 refers then to those faithful who will still be living at the time of the terrible cosmic dissolutions of the Last Day that enacts the wrath of God and of the Lamb. Interestingly, the tribes of Dan and Ephraim are not mentioned here, probably because these tribes were infamous for their idolatry. If this exclusion is deliberate, the 144,000 probably represent those Christians alive at the "Day of the Lord" who have had no connection with idolatry or the Antichrist.

The second vision (Rev 7:9-17). This vision pictures a great international multitude clad in white, with palms of victory in their hands. They stand before the throne of God and the Lamb. It proclaims and praises the salvation (not victory) belonging to God and the Lamb. The Greek word *sōtēria* means the total well-being of people. *Sōtēria* (salvation) is found in Revelation only in hymnic passages that refer to eschatological, final salvation (7:10; 12:10; 19:1). In the soteriological hymn 12:10b-12, the term is used parallel to and synonymous with the empire of God (*basileia tou theou*). The official source of such total well-being, peace, and salvation, according to the political ideology of the time, was the Roman emperor. In contrast, those who stand before the throne acknowledge God and the Lamb as the ultimate source of all well-being and salvation. The heavenly world confirms the acclamation of the eschatological victors by responding with "Amen" and a hymn similar to the hymns in chapters 4 and 5. This doxology refers to the thanksgiving in 4:9. God the creator wills the total well-being of all. Thus, the royal throne room, the heavenly temple, and the eschatological New Jerusalem coalesce here into a single vision of a renewed world of salvation and well-being brought about by the presence of God and Christ.

The second vision receives a lengthy interpretation—a rhetorical device of the author to underline the importance of a visionary account. In contrast to the 144,000 who represent Christians still living but protected in the last days of cosmic dissolution, the vision of the international multitude before the throne appears to symbolize those who have endured and survived the great tribulation that precedes the Last Day. That the time of eschatological tribulation is coextensive with the everyday troubles of the Asian communities has already been stated in 1:9. There John has asserted that, as their comrade, he shares in the time of tribulation. The Synoptic apocalypse (Mark 13 and its parallels) understands the sufferings of this time of eschatological tribulation, which are symbolically narrated in the first five seal visions, as the birth pangs of a renewed world free from evil.

The paradoxical image of "having washed their robes in the blood of the Lamb" may refer to the baptism of the great multitude. It could also allude to their present experience of suffering and violence at the hands of the anti-human and antidivine powers that have also caused the violent death of Christ. Their number, however, is not necessarily limited to Christians but could include all those who have suffered the violence of the great tribulation, war, hunger, pestilence, death, and persecution.

Eschatological salvation and well-being are proclaimed both from the perspective of God and from a human perspective. The Shekinah-radiance of God's presence in the midst of the people who worship and acclaim the One on the throne is symbolized by the "tent," the tabernacle of God's presence that will be spread over them. The total well-being and salvation of the people of God are painted in colors and tones derived from the prophetic promises to the exiles of Israel returning from Babylon. Those who participate in eschatological salvation will never again experience physical hardship, deprivation, hunger, or thirst. As their shepherd and ruler, Christ will satisfy them from the wellsprings of eternal life. All suffering, tears, and mourning will cease.

According to Revelation, final salvation does not pertain just to the soul and spiritual realities. Rather, it means abolishment of all dehumanization and suffering as well as restoration of the fullness of human well-being. The vision and promise of such ultimate well-being thus are clearly intended to fortify those who face the great tribulation with all its sufferings, including war, hunger, inflation, pestilence, persecution, and death. This vision of eschatological well-being and salvation is the answer to the outcry of those seeking justice and revenge for the destruction of their lives.

After the interlude of chapter 7, which envisions the eschatological protection and salvation of the people of God, the opening of the seventh seal seems almost anticlimactic. Its delay is, however, a brilliant rhetorical device for introducing a striking contrast and deepening suspense. The half hour of breathless silence impressively contrasts with the acclamation and hymn of chapter 7 as well as with the deafening noise of the thunders, voices, and earthquakes of 8:5. At the same time, the seventh seal vision prepares structurally during this interval of silence for the blowing of the seven trumpets reminding the audience of the content of the scroll whose seals are now all opened.

Revelation 8:2—9:21
Six Trumpets Announcing the
Eschatological Plagues

The literary structure of the trumpet septet parallels the seven-series of the seal visions. Like the first four seals, the first four trumpets follow a definite, parallel pattern. The fifth and sixth trumpets in turn correspond in form to the fifth and sixth seal visions insofar as they do not follow the same pattern but are elaborated in different ways. The eagle's (or vulture's) proclamation of the woes marks a formal break in the trumpet series. Just as the interlude of chapter 7 postpones the opening of the seventh seal, so also does the interlude of chapters 10–11 delay the victory blast of the seventh trumpet.

One can comprehend the artful composition of this whole section only when one recognizes the author's literary technique of *intercalation* (sandwiching or interlocking). The author utilizes this method of intercalation in the following way: He narrates two episodes or two formal units (*A* and *A'*) that essentially belong together. Between these two units, he intercalates another unit different in form and content from the other two (*B*). As we have seen, the author uses this method of intercalation in structuring the introduction of the book insofar as he inserts the epistolary form into the prophetic form of introduction. In a similar way, the author sandwiches the heavenly liturgy in 8:3-5 (B) between the appearance of the angels with the trumpets in 8:2 (A) and the execution of the plagues in 8:6—9:21a (A').

John, however, links the trumpet series with the following visions by way of a double intercalation, insofar as he clearly marks Rev 10:1—11:14 as an interlude which is inserted into the septet of the trumpet visions (8:6—9:21a; 10:1—11:14b; 11:15-19a'). Simultaneously, the section 10:1—11:14 connects with chapters 12–14 in that it refers to the same time period and the same kind of persecution by the beast as chapters 12–14 do. By introducing this visionary unit as the "little scroll," the author makes it parallel to, as well as envelops it in, the seven-sealed scroll which the Lamb receives in chapter 5. Thus, compositionally the author, through intercalation, forges links between the small prophetic scroll and the following visions (10:1—11:14a; 11:15-19b; 12:12-14a'). Moreover, the pronouncement of the eagle's woe also interweaves the small scroll with the trumpet series of visions insofar as the eagle announces the first woe as early as 9:12 and the second as having occurred already in 11:14. The third woe (12:12a) refers to chapters 12–13. All three woes speak of the same demonic and satanic powers of evil.

The trumpet visions also perform a literary function within the book of Revelation as a whole. Revelation 5:1 specifies that writings appeared "inside and on the back" of the scroll. After the Lamb has opened the seals and inaugurated the end time, the visionary narrative dramatizes the contents of the scroll. Insofar as the trumpet and bowl series of visions recall the pattern of the Egyptian plagues and parallel each other, they seem to refer to the two written sides of the scroll. As becomes clear in the bowl septet, they tell how God executes wrath and judgment. Yet just as God had inflicted the Egyptian plagues in order to make possible the exodus of Israel from Egypt, so the cosmic plagues of the trumpet series and the bowl series execute the judgment of God over the cosmos, enabling the liberation of the Christian community from the oppression of Babylon/Rome.

The prelude 8:2-5 introduces the seven angels of the Presence or the seven archangels. They are probably identical with the angels who in 15:5—19:10 pour out the bowls of the wrath of God. The trumpets, which are given to these angels, carry many symbolic allusions. Trumpets were sounded to announce war and victory, to call people together, to celebrate feast days, and to herald the coronation of a king. Here they call to mind especially those eschatological connotations which the Hebrew Bible and early Christian writings associate with the sound of trumpets. They herald the Day of the Lord (Zeph 1:14ff), announce the day of judgment (4 Ezra 6:23), or proclaim the resurrection of the dead and the dawn of a new order (1 Thess 4:16; 1 Cor 15:52; Matt 24:31).

After the introduction of the seven trumpet angels, the interlude 8:3-5 focuses our attention on the heavenly liturgy of wrath and judgment. A priest-angel adds incense to the prayers of the saints upon the golden altar before the throne of God. The prayers of the saints become like burning charcoal upon which the grains of incense are laid, causing their smoke to rise up before God's throne. Whereas in 5:8 the bowls of incense that are used in the hymnic liturgy celebrating the Lamb's enthronement to kingship symbolize the prayers of the saints, here the prayers of the saints kindle and sustain the fire of the altar that signifies God's wrath and judgment. Like the outcry of the martyrs in 6:9-11, so the prayers of the saints who are persecuted demand justice and seek to bring about the judgment of God.

Although the form of the first four trumpet visions (8:6-12) parallels that of the first four seal visions, the contents of these visions clearly differ. They bring destruction not just upon the Roman Empire, but upon all elements of the cosmos—upon earth, sea, and sky. The symbol of fire reoccurs in all the first four trumpet visions. It recalls the same fire that the priest-angel has cast down on earth and signifies the wrath and judgment of God. This judgment affects the whole cosmos: the earth, the sea, the inland waters, and the heavenly bodies. The destruction of the four dimensions of the world, however, is not total since the plagues of the trumpets destroy only one-third of the world. Moreover, just as the Israelites were spared from the Egyptian plagues, so the cosmic plagues will not touch those who have the protection of God's seal.

The fifth and the sixth trumpet visions are distinct in structure and content. In contrast to the first four trumpets, they do not set in motion the destruction of the cosmic order. Rather, they reveal the activity of the demonic-satanic power which tortures and kills one-third of humanity. Whereas the fifth trumpet clearly refers to the events of the first woe, some questions remain as to whether the second woe refers to the events symbolically narrated in 9:13—11:14 or only to those told in the vision about the two prophets (11:3-4).

The fifth trumpet vision (9:1-12) displays the repulsive image of mythical locusts coming from the abyss which was opened by the angel-star fallen, like Satan, from heaven (cf. Luke 10:18). The plague of the locusts with the power of scorpions derives from Exod 10:1-20. Already before Revelation was written, this plague had been eschatologically interpreted as a portent of the destruction coming with the dawn of the Day of the Lord. The bizarre description of the locusts as horse-shaped, long-haired flying insects with scorpion tails, wearing golden crowns above human faces that are marred by lions' teeth, should not be allegorized. Rather, it should simply be seen as an exaggerated, repulsive depiction of unnatural, demonic power.

The Greek name of the locusts' king, Apollyon, probably engages in derogatory wordplay on the god Apollo, since the locust was one of his symbols. The Roman emperor Domitian also claimed to be an incarnation of this god.

If such a pun is intended, then the author ironically asserts that the destructive hosts of the abyss have as their king the Roman emperor who claims to be the divine incarnation of Apollo.

The sixth trumpet plague (9:13-21) presents an even more repulsive picture and frightening scene. The torment of the locusts gives way to the massacre of one-third of all human beings by fire-breathing mythological horse-monsters. In 8:3-5, the introductory reference to the golden altar alludes to the heavenly liturgy of judgment. In addition, the reference to the four angels brings to mind the four angels who stay the destructive winds in 7:1-3. In contrast, the four angels are loosed here to kill one-third of the world's population. Their destructive power is signified by innumerable squadrons of cavalry.

It must not be overlooked, however, that not the riders but the horses execute the plague insofar as out of their mouths fire, smoke, and brimstone issue to cause destruction. Whereas the mouths of these mythic monsterlike horses have the power to kill, their serpent tails have the power to harm. The concluding verses 9:20-21 indicate, however, that John writes this grotesque and brutal vision not for cruelty's sake but rather for the sake of exhortation to repentance. Following the pattern of the Exodus plagues inflicted upon the Egyptians, the author's rhetorical vision stresses that those who were killed did not repent from their idolatry nor from the pagan practices associated with it.

The examination of these last two plague visions makes it clear how disastrous it would be to misunderstand Revelation as an accurate description of what has already happened in the time of John or as an elaborate prediction of events which will actually happen in the eschatological future. Revelation functions neither as an accurate transcript of divine information nor as a factual prediction of future eschatological events. Instead, it must be read as a rhetorical work of vision written in the language of image and myth. As such, it could be likened to today's literature warning against ecological and atomic destruction.

Present-day futuristic accounts portraying atomic warfare, ecological devastation, or scientific cloning do not intend to predict or accurately describe the future. Rather, they offer a fictional projection of what might be if the industrialized nations do not halt their military expansion or their technological exploitation of the earth. The terrible visions of such literature that portray a totally manipulated and dehumanized future seek to shock us out of our current lethargy. They are based on our present knowledge of the destructive potential of nuclear power, and they envision the worst possibilities for devastation. Their rhetoric seeks to spur us on to cut military spending and to stop nuclear deployment.

In a similar fashion, Revelation's mythological rhetoric represents the repulsive and grotesque powers of Satan and the abyss in order to shock the audience to repent from idolatry and to reject completely destructive powers. At the same time, Revelation's rhetoric seeks to engender trust and confidence in God's justice and powers of well-being even though experience and evidence seem to mock such hope and faith.

D. The Bitter-sweet Scroll:
"War" against the Community
Revelation 10:1—15:4

Introduction

Anyone attempting to construct a chronological or even a logical sequence of events in Revelation must once again give up in despair when analyzing the central chapters of the book. Whereas the seven-cycles of the messages, seals, and trumpets at least follow a clearly marked numerical pattern and build on each other, no such pattern emerges in Rev 10:1—14:20. Several scholars have attempted to establish a series of seven unnumbered visions, but their proposals differ widely. Moreover, one can assume that the author would have been capable of writing another series of seven in clear and explicit fashion if that had been his intention; therefore, the visionary sequence Rev 10:1—14:20 was in all likelihood not conceived as a series of seven visions.

Since in Rev 10:1—14:20 John does not employ the literary technique of numerical structure, one must pay special attention to other literary marks which he used elsewhere in Revelation—such literary techniques as intercalation, cross-referencing, and symbolic contrasts. In 10:1ff the description and dramatic setting of the "little scroll" which is open clearly contrasts with the sevenfold scroll of chapter 5 which is introduced as sealed. Moreover, the prophetic commissioning of John and the characterization of the angel in 10:1 refer the audience to the prophetic call and "humanlike" figure in the inaugural vision in chapter 1. Last and most important, the references to the beast and its mark (11:7; 13:1; 13:6f; 14:9; 15:2; cf. 14:1) as well as to the duration of the activity of the Christians and their oppressors (11:2, 3; 12:15; 13:6) cover the same time period. The symbolic contrast of the beast and the Lamb as well as that of the beastly homage and the divine liturgy also indicate that the same actors determine chapters 11–14.

As I have argued, the sevenfold sealed scroll taken over by the Lamb narrates symbolically the eschatological end-time tribulation and the final cataclysms of the Lord's Day from a "heavenly perspective." The open little scroll taken and eaten by John draws our attention to the situation of oppression on earth. The visions that follow depict the eschatological struggles of the followers of the Lamb on earth against the idolatrous and destructive powers of the beast. Perhaps John has not communicated these visions in the form of a septet because he understood the number seven to be the number of heaven in contrast with the number six, which is the number of the beast.

As I have already pointed out, the little prophetic scroll is interconnected with the preceding section of the trumpet series through the literary means of intercalation and double inclusion. Chapters 10 and 11 are clearly marked as an interlude before the blast of the last trumpet. As such, they have the same structural function within Revelation as the interlude of chapter 7. Not only do they refer to the situation and time period of chapters 12–14, but they also can be seen as a prelude to the coming chapters. Thus the following *double* inclusion can be recognized: *a* (sixth trumpet), *b* (interlude of chaps. 10 and 11), *a'* (seventh trumpet), and *b'* (chaps. 12–13).

The vision of the 144,000 on Mount Zion (14:1-5, *a*) is followed by the announcement of the bowl seven-series and of the destruction of Babylon (14:6-13, *b*). It is in turn complemented by the double vision of the double eschatological harvest (14:14-20, *a'*) which in turn leads to the introduction of the seven angels with the bowls of God's wrath (15:1, *b'*). These visions of chapters 11–14 climax in the heavenly homage of the victors to God's justice (15:2-3, *a''*). Their hymnic homage serves at the same time as a prelude to and interpretation of the last cosmic plague-series (15:6ff, *b''*). Thus the central section of Revelation can be divided as follows: *C* (9:13-21), *D* (10:1—11:14), *C* (11:15-19), *D* (12:1—14:5), *C'* (14:6-13), *D* (14:14-20), *C'* (15:1), *D* (15:2-5), *C'* (15:6ff). (See the complete outline in Part One, B., 3.) Such a literary analysis of the narrative structure sheds light on the rhetorical and thereby theological functions of individual sections.

Revelation 10:1—11:13
The Self-understanding and Task
of the Christian Seer

The interlude, Rev 10:1—11:13, not only coheres structurally but also stylistically insofar as the "I saw" of 10:1 characterizes the whole section as a single vision. This fact is obscured by the present chapter divisions, especially when the fact that the enumeration of verses and chapters was added at a much later date is overlooked. The unified vision of the interlude inserted into the trumpet series consists of the following sections: the angel and the thunders (10:1-4); the oath of the angel referring to the seventh trumpet (10:5-7); the taking and eating of the little scroll (10:8-10); the renewed prophetic commissioning of John (10:11—11:2); the power and fate of the two witnesses (11:3-12); and finally, the summary statement about the effects of the whole vision (11:13-14). An analysis of these six sections follows:

The first section. The vision 10:1-4 introduces the open little scroll, placed not in the outstretched palm of God but in that of a mighty angel. The appearance of this angel alludes to some of the features of the Christ-figure in the inaugural vision of 1:12-20. The downward movement of this powerful angel focuses the audience's attention again on the earth. The rainbow around the angel's head may be a sign of God's covenant with creation (Gen 9:13). The cloud and the pillars of fire in turn evoke the Exodus and Sinai covenant with Israel (Exod 13:21ff; 19:16ff).

The figure of the seven thunders is accompanied by the command to "seal up" what they have said. The possible meaning of this injundiary has puzzled many minds, and the question of the thunders' function remains far from clear. Thunder with lightning, etc., in Revelation expresses theophany (cf. Rev 4:5; 8:5; 11:19; 16:18) or characterizes a heavenly voice (cf. Rev 6:1; 14:2; 19:6). In all likelihood Psalm 29 influenced the figure of the seven thunders since this psalm understands thunder as "the voice of God." The text repeats this phrase seven times in order to underline the power and splendor of God's voice. But why must the seer seal what the sevenfold thundering voice of God reveals? John may allude here to a traditional Synoptic saying which states that only God knows the day or hour of the parousia (Mark 13:32; Matt 24:36). The figure of the thunders and the prohibition to write are then best understood as a literary means to stress that no one can know the day and hour of the end.

The second section. The oath of the angel that "there should be no delay" and that at the sounding of the seventh trumpet the mystery of God will be fulfilled (10:5-7) supports this interpretation. The section probably has Dan 12:1-7 as a literary backdrop. After Daniel receives instruction to seal the book until the time of the end (12:4), someone asks: "How long until these wonders take place?" In response to this rhetorical question, the angel swears by God who "lives forever" that "a time and two times and half a time" have to pass (cf. Rev 12:14) until "the one who crushes the power of the holy people meets the end" (Dan 12:7). In Revelation, the same time period (i.e., forty-two months) refers to the time of the Christian community as well as to its persecution by the beast.

As we shall see, the seventh trumpet proclaims the realization and extension of God's rule over the whole world as the mystery that was revealed as "good news" to the prophets. The expression "mystery" and the explanation "the secret plan or decree of God" may interpret the symbolization of the seven thunders. When the seventh trumpet is sounded, then this mystery revealed only to John will be made public. Since this seventh trumpet is already sounded toward the center rather than at the end of Revelation, the author indicates thereby that the narrative sequence of the book's visions is not chronological. The vision of the seventh trumpet thus appears to speak about the same final eschatological salvation that is also the focus of the last chapters of Revelation.

The third section. After the pressing question of "How long?" is clarified, the attention of the audience shifts back to the little scroll lying in the outstretched hand of the angel (10:8-10). Ezek 2:8—3:3 provides the background for this prophetic, symbolic action. Like Ezekiel, John is told to take and eat the scroll, an action which probably means to become aware of the scroll's contents, to internalize and appropriate them. As the "word of God," referring to God's eschatological salvation, the little scroll tastes sweet (cf. Ps 19:10); but in contrast with Ezekiel, it becomes bitter when digested. Earlier, at the blast of the third trumpet, a third of the waters had turned bitter "and many died of the water because it was made bitter." This bitter and poisonous water symbolizes death. Similarly, the "turning bitter of the scroll" appears to spell death. The following chapter 11 draws out the "sweetness" of the prophetic word by promising divine protection for the true worshipers, and at the same time it turns "bitter" when depicting the prophetic witnesses as being killed in the war with the beast.

The fourth section. This rhetorical stress on the "double" taste of the small scroll corresponds to the twofold commissioning of the prophet (10:11—11:2). The injunction to prophesy against many nations is phrased in the typical Danielic formula. The addition of "kings" indicates that the author refers also to the visions following chapter 11. These chapters depict the nations as raging against God and God's worshipers and the kings of the earth as following after the great Babylon/Rome.

In 11:1-2, the heavenly voice instructs John not only to prophesy but also to perform a prophetic sign-action which seems patterned after Ezek 40:3; but whereas in Ezekiel (as in Rev 21:15) the measuring of Jerusalem symbolizes restoration, the symbolic action enjoined upon John in 11:1-2 probably entails protection of what is not yet destroyed. Some exegetes therefore suggest that John here appropriates for his purposes a Zealot oracle which was in circulation before the destruction of Jerusalem by the Romans. Yet, one must ask why John would have incorporated such a Zealot source since he was writing long after the destruction of Jerusalem and the temple. Moreover, if such a tradition were incorporated here, its function and meaning must still be derived from its present context in Revelation.

With this symbolic action John probably intends to dramatize his prophetic announcements just as Israel's prophets did with their sign-actions. The prophetic action of measuring must be understood in a symbolic-metaphorical rather than in a literal way since the temple and the city of Jerusalem are already in ruins at the writing of Revelation. The measuring here probably symbolizes eschatological protection and strengthening of the Christian community just as the measuring in 1 Enoch 61:1-5 does. Those who are eschatologically protected are the priestly worshipers of God. In contrast with those who are the true worshipers of God, the court of the Gentiles will not be protected but is to be excluded from eschatological salvation. Rev 11:2b seems a close parallel to Luke 21:24, but it replaces the Lukan mention of Jerusalem with the expression "holy city" and describes the length of the "time of the Gentiles" with the Danielic number "forty and two months."

Since the author uses the name "Jerusalem" just for the New Jerusalem, his characterization of the city as the "holy city" seems to refer to neither the eschatological nor the historical Jerusalem, which in 11:8 is called "the great city." If the expression "holy city" means the same circle of persons as the figures "temple, altar, and worshipers," then 11:2 speaks of the Christian community. The symbolic rhetoric of 11:1-2 thus promises that as the true priestly worshipers, Christians will be eschatologically strengthened and protected in the end time. In contrast, the Gentiles will be excluded from final salvation because they have persecuted Christians. Rev 11:1-2 is therefore best understood as a prophetic announcement of reversal. Christians who *now* suffer the oppressions and persecutions of the nations will be eschatologically protected in the end while the nations will suffer the eschatological plagues and punishments of God's wrath.

The fifth section. Revelation 11:3-12 speaks symbolically of the witness and fate of Christian prophets. Insofar as the vision of the two witnesses does not have its own introduction, this section belongs formally to the commissioning vision of 10:11—11:2 and thus also functions as an overture to the visions that follow. During the period when Christians are downtrodden by the nations, the figures of the two eschatological witnesses representing Christian prophets call the peoples of the earth to repentance and penitence. Rev 11:3-12 therefore seems to expand and elaborate on the prophetic commissioning in 10:11—11:2. The time of prophetic activity which is symbolically narrated in the activity and fate of the two witnesses corresponds to the time in which the Christian community is persecuted.

After verse 11:3 has announced the power and duration of the two witnesses' activity, Rev 11:4 indicates their identity. Rev 11:5-6 metaphorically elaborates their prophetic power and protection by God whereas Rev 11:7-12 describes their fate as similar to that of Christ. By imaging the two witnesses as olive trees and lamp stands, as well as by interpreting the great city "spiritually," John communicates that he is intentionally using symbolic-theological language. Attempting to identify the two witnesses as historical personages, or to interpret every feature of the vision in a historical-allegorical way, misses John's hermeneutical intention and brings unsatisfactory results.

The images of olive tree and temple menorah probably derive from Zech 4:2, where they symbolize the kingship of Zerubbabel and the high priesthood of Joshua. The image of the temple menorah also refers to Revelation's inaugural vision, where in 1:20 John's interpretation identifies the seven lamp stands as representing the Christian community. Rev 1:6 and 5:10 have also stressed the royal/priestly character of Christians. That two witnesses are mentioned rather than one could allude either to the injunction of Deut 19:15 (cf. John 8:17) that requires at least two persons to provide valid witness, or to the commissioning in Luke 10:1 where the disciples are sent out in pairs, or to both traditions. Most probably John had the latter passage in mind because his assertion that no one is able to harm the two witnesses seems to refer to Luke's Gospel. According to Luke 10:19, the disciples are promised that nothing will harm them, not even serpents, not scorpions, nor "all the powers of the enemy." This phrase thus seems to express the meaning of the symbolic action of "measuring" in 11:1.

The royal/priestly witnesses are depicted as endowed with the power of Elijah (fire from their mouths, power to shut the sky) and of Moses (power over the waters and reference to "every plague"), both of whom were expected to return as the final eschatological prophets. The two symbolic figures representing Christian prophets and witnesses have the power "to smite the earth with every plague." This statement appears to imply that Christian prophets participate in bringing about the eschatological plagues (cf. the outcry of the victims for justice in 6:10 and the "prayer of the saints" in 5:8 and 8:2ff). If so, the symbolic rhetoric of the text asserts that although Christians will be persecuted and oppressed, no one will be able to halt their prophetic witness nor their call to repentance. Rather, injuries inflicted upon them increase the wrath of God and the eschatological plagues.

Attempts to puzzle out each statement of 11:7-12 in an allegorical fashion have produced exegetical confusion with respect to the meaning of the text; however, the basic outline of Revelation's rhetorical symbolization is clear: The eschatological fate of Christian prophets and witnesses is very much like that of their Lord. After they complete their task, the beast ascending from the abyss (9:1; 13:1) will fight, conquer, and kill them (12:17; 13:7, 15). Thus the depiction of the two witnesses' activity interlinks chapter 11 with the following visions of chapters 12–13. The expression "great city" that, according to prophetic (not allegorical) insight, is the moral and spiritual equivalent of Sodom and Egypt, may allude to the oppressive power of Rome, since the Romans were legally responsible for the execution of Jesus. In any case, the death, resurrection, and exaltation of the two witnesses mirror the fate of Jesus. Although Christian prophets and witnesses stand eschatologically protected and cannot be prohibited from completing their mission, they will have to suffer death just as their Lord had to die. Just as the Lamb was made alive again, they too are promised resurrection and exaltation.

The sixth section. The visionary narrative elaborating the task and witness of the Christian prophets concludes with a cosmic earthquake which causes the partial destruction of the great city and its inhabitants; but while the cosmic plagues (6:12; 8:5; 11:19; 16:18) do not bring about repentance, the prophetic witness of Christians, even unto death, does. Nine-tenths of the nations and citizens of the world will repent and "give God honor." Since the preaching of wrath upon the citizens of the world permeates Revelation, scholars argue that 11:13 does not suggest that the nations repent but only that they are smitten with fear. Yet, the expression "they praised the God of heaven" is repeated in 14:7 and announced as the content of the gospel that is proclaimed to all peoples of the earth. Thus, 11:13 seems to anticipate the pronouncement of 15:3-4 that all the nations will come and worship God. It is crucial to recognize that Revelation's rhetoric of judgment expresses hope for the conversion of nine-tenths of the nations in response to Christian witness and preaching. Otherwise, one will not understand that the author advocates a theology of justice rather than a theology of hate and resentment.

Revelation 11:14-19
The Eternal Kingdom of
God and Christ

The statement in 11:14 regarding the second and third woes refers to the fifth trumpet (9:12) and thereby marks 10:1—11:13 structurally as an interlude within the trumpet septet. At the same time, the seventh trumpet vision functions as a prelude to the series of visions depicting the war of the beasts against the saints. In addition, the oath of the angel in 10:1ff has already assured the audience that the seventh trumpet will announce the final end and ultimate salvation. The seventh trumpet thus functions rhetorically to anticipate the visions of salvation in Revelation 21–22.

The eschatological victory hymn 11:17-18 announces the judgment and reign of God and Christ. God will punish the destroyers of the earth and reward not only Christians but all those who have repented and acknowledged God. God's judgment and empire mean the liberation of the earth from all destructive powers, especially from those of Babylon/Rome (19:2); and at the same time, it brings about the renewal of the covenant with creation. The destructive powers of the nations have provoked the wrath of God, which is elaborately depicted in the eschatological plague visions. Nevertheless, the ultimate goal of the plague visions is not destruction but the liberation of all humanity and of the whole earth from oppressive and destructive powers. This is the hope that John's rhetorical vision places before Christians who are told simultaneously that they must suffer oppression and persecution through the hands of the nations.

Revelation 12:1-17
The Woman and the Dragon

Chapter 12 takes the form of an inclusion. Between the great portent of the glorious woman and the powerful dragon (12:1-6) on the one hand and the vision of the dragon's persecution of the woman (12:13-17) on the other, John inserts the vision about war in heaven waged by the dragon (12:7-12). He first draws the audience's attention to the glorious sign in heaven, but at the end of each section he shifts the focus again toward the earth. The whole vision appears to be a mythological elaboration of the eschatological war-motif already sounded in Rev 11:7.

The myth of the queen of heaven with the divine child was internationally known at the time of John. Variations appear in Babylonia, Egypt, Greece, Asia Minor, and especially in the texts about astral religion. Elements of this myth are: the goddess and the divine child, the great red dragon and his enmity to mother and child, and the motif of the protection of mother and child. Revelation 12 also incorporates these elements. As in other versions of the myth, the dragon seeks the child not yet born in order to devour and kill him. The dragon therefore pursues the pregnant woman for the child she carries. In other forms of the myth, the woman is either carried away to give birth in a protected place or she gives birth in a miraculous way and escapes the onslaught of the dragon together with the newborn. In Revelation 12 the child is exalted to heaven while the woman is carried to the desert for the sake of her own protection.

Some features of this international myth appear also in the Roman imperial cult. A coin of Pergamum, for instance, shows the goddess Roma with the divine emperor. In the cities of Asia Minor Roma, the queen of heaven, was worshiped as the mother of the gods. Her oldest temple stood in Smyrna. Her imperial child was celebrated as the world's savior, incarnation of the sun-god, Apollo. John probably intends such an allusion to the imperial cult and the goddess Roma insofar as he pictures the woman clothed with the sun as the anti-image of Babylon, the symbol of the world power of his day and its allies (chaps. 17–18).

John, however, reinterprets this international ancient myth in terms of Jewish expectations. His emphasis on the travail of the woman does not derive from the ancient pagan myth but takes inspiration from the Hebrew Bible's image of Israel-Zion in messianic times. The vision of the woman in labor pains alludes to Israel-Zion seen in Isaiah (26:16-27; 54:1; 66:7-9) as a mother awaiting the delivery of the messianic age (cf. Mic 4:9-10). With the symbolic language of Isaiah and the ancient pagan myth, John invokes the image of the messianic child being born accompanied by the birth pangs of the messianic woes. In Revelation, this child without question represents Jesus Christ, who is exalted and receives the powers of messianic kingship (cf. Ps 2:8; Rev 11:18; 19:15). The "birth of the Messiah" refers here not to the historical birth of Jesus but to his exaltation and enthronement as the "firstborn of the dead" and as the "beginning of the new creation." God has prevented the dragon from devouring the child.

The figure of the dragon, serpent, crocodile, or sea monster is also familiar from ancient mythology and from the Hebrew Bible. In Jewish writings, it frequently serves as a symbol of an oppressor nation like Egypt (Ps 74:14) and its ruler, Pharaoh (Ezek 32:2ff), or like Syria and Babylon (Isa 27:1). Daniel uses this symbol for the last great antidivine nation and its ruler, the opponent of Israel (7:1-7). Within this symbolic context, readers can understand the red dragon as the ultimate foe of the people of God.

The woman, whose fate is announced in 12:6 and expanded on in the concluding section of the vision, has been subject to various interpretations. Scholars have proposed that this glorious figure represents either the figure of Israel-Zion in the Hebrew Bible, or the heavenly church, or the historical mother of Jesus, Mary. In any case, it seems obvious that the vision intends a multivalent mythological symbolization of transpersonal divine realities. In the context of Revelation, the woman clothed with the sun who is in labor is best understood as the messianic community. It is nourished by God in the desert during the time of persecution (cf. Dan 7:25; Rev 11:2; 13:5). The desert recalls Israel's forty-year journey through the desert (Exod 19:4, 16). If the figure of the woman in chapter 12 is an image of the messianic community, then like the vision of the sealing of the 144,000 (chap. 7) and the prophetic sign-action of measuring the priestly worshipers (11:1-2), it promises that Christians will be eschatologically protected and saved, although the war waged with the beast might harm and even kill them (12:13-17).

The central section, Revelation 12:7-12, reveals the deepest cause for the persecution and oppression experienced by Christians in the time of John. Its mythological symbolization of the "war in heaven" serves to explain in the language of Jewish myth the role of Satan or the Devil. This accuser and prosecutor of the faithful for a short time has the opportunity to exercise his power on earth, which is Satan's domain since the exaltation of Christ. The image of "war in heaven" is intertwined with that of a court trial in which Satan functions as the prosecutor and Michael as the defender of God's people.

The victory hymn of the heavenly court in 12:10-12 is inserted here in order to proclaim the reality of the salvation, power, and empire of God and

Christ. Its rhetoric asserts that the witnesses have won the victory because they have honored their redemption through Christ when they did not surrender even in the face of death; therefore, great rejoicing and feasting take place in the heavenly world whereas Satan's expulsion means woe for the earth. The third woe announces to the world and its inhabitants that Satan exercises his oppressive power on earth.

Revelation 12:18—14:5
The Cult of the Beast and
the Followers of the Lamb

This section is again composed in the form of an inclusion: two mythical beasts rise up, one coming from the sea (13:1-10 [*a*]) and the "other" arising from the land (13:11-18 [*b*]). The second beast in turn is replaced by the Lamb standing on Mount Zion (14:1-5 [*A'*]) who in turn is the mirror image of the first wild beast from the sea. John's depiction of the appearance of each of these three *visionary figures* concludes with an explicit prophetic interpretation in the form of a warning (13:10), an apocalyptic parable (13:18), or a theological identification of the Lamb's followers (14:4-5).

The language for the mythical symbolizations of the two beasts derives from the primeval myth of the two monsters who were separated. It also contains many direct allusions to Daniel. The monster Leviathan was to live in the abyss of the ocean, whereas Behemoth was to dwell on the dry land. According to Jewish folklore, these two primeval monsters have messianic eschatological functions (2 Bar. 29:4, 8; 4 Ezra 6:49ff). The Danielic overtones of the section suggest a political interpretation of the two beasts, since such a political interpretation of the Danielic four beasts was well known in the Jewish literature of the time.

The statement of 12:18 forms a bridge that links the conclusion of 12:17 with the new image of the wild beast from the sea (13:1). It therefore functions as an introduction to the whole section, which begins with the image of the dragon standing at the shore of the sea and concludes with the image of the Lamb standing on Mount Zion. The whole section thus expands upon the announcement of 12:17 that the dragon wages war with the rest of the woman's offspring, who clearly are characterized as Christians. The rage of Satan against the woman, who symbolizes the messianic community, fuels the rage of the nations (11:18), who are said to destroy the earth. It is important, however, to keep in mind that John repeatedly insists that the cruel war waged by the antidivine powers does not prove the powerlessness of God and Christ. It also does not express the positive will of God. The apocalyptic expression "it was given" repeatedly makes the point that God permits and tolerates this life-destroying war, but only for a very short time.

REVELATION 13:1-10
THE PROPHETIC UNMASKING OF
ROMAN IMPERIAL POWER

The first wild beast emerges from the sea where the dragon stands. (The reading "I was standing . . ." is best understood as a later variant manuscript reading.) The seashore envisioned here is probably that of the Mediterranean Sea with Rome geographically located on its opposite shore. To people of the province Asia, the beast's arrival might have appeared to represent the proconsul emerging from the sea at the arrival for his annual visit in Ephesus. Similarly, according to the Jewish apocalypse of Ezra, the eagle symbolizing Rome comes from the sea (4 Ezra 11:1). However, the sea itself has not just a geographical meaning but also a mythological significance. For according to ancient beliefs, the sea symbolizes chaos, evil, and demonic powers (cf. Rev 9:2; 11:7). Israel's God is praised for having slain sea monsters (Ps 74:13-14; Isa 27:1). All four of the beasts representing empires in Daniel come from the sea.

The monster emerging from the sea displays ten horns adorned with diadems, seven heads like the dragon, and one huge mouth uttering blasphemies. The depiction of this bizarre creature combines in surrealistic fashion all the features of the four beasts of Daniel 7, which represent different kingdoms and political powers. If Revelation takes its meaning from Daniel 7, then the beast embodies all political powers of the time. Combining the features of the four beasts, which in Daniel portray the sequence of four world empires, the seven-headed and ten-horned monster stands for total oppressive dominion and dehumanizing power. The monster's might, however, is not self-generated; but, rather, it has received its kingship and sovereignty from Satan, whose throne according to Revelation is located in Pergamum (2:13).

This beast not only exercises its dominion as the viceroy of Satan's powers, but its image also appears to be the parodic mirror image of the Lamb. For instance, one of the beast's heads looks "as though slaughtered to death," the same Greek expression that was used to characterize the Lamb. The mortal wound of the monster may also allude to the Nero legend. Rumor had it that Nero did not really die but would return with the Parthian army to take revenge. Moreover, the author interprets the healing of the beast's deadly wound in 13:14 as signifying resurrection from death. In addition, as Christ shares the throne of God (3:21; chap. 5), so does the monster share that of Satan. Furthermore, the monster's blasphemous names parody the unknown name of Christ who is the Word of God (19:12). Finally, just as the members of Christ's royal/priestly community come from all nations, tongues, and peoples, so do the followers of the beast. The whole world prostrates in adoration before Satan and the beast (13:4) acknowledging and praising them in the language of the Psalms: "Yahweh, who can compare with you?" (Ps 35:10).

The beast directs all its energies against God and the dwellings of God's power. This monster characterized as Antichrist cannot but wage war against the saints and win victory over them. The time of persecution and suffering caused by the monster coincides with the time of the two witnesses (Rev 11:17) as well as with the duration of the woman's (12:6, 10) and the true worshipers' protection (11:2). These narrative symbolizations prophetically illuminate in different ways the same "last time" of tribulation before the eschatological end. In addition, the multivalent imagery of Revelation clearly receives concrete political focus in John's rhetorical symbolization. John does not speak in general terms about human suffering and demonic reality, but he instead prophetically identifies the oppression of Christians and other peoples as engendered by the political usurpation of God's power.

Therefore, John ends this vision of the grotesque monster representing political imperial power by reiterating the call to allegiance with which he has concluded each of the seven messages to the churches: Pay attention! If necessary, Christians must realize their loyal resistance and faithful steadfastness by going into captivity or being executed. No peaceful coexistence can exist between the worshipers of Satan and the followers of the monster on the one hand and those advocating God's and Christ's power and sovereignty on the other. The war between the monster from the sea and the Lamb spells total warfare. Revelation's symbolic rhetoric is absolute: one decides either for God or Satan, for the Lamb or the monster, for Christ or Antichrist. No compromise is possible.

REVELATION 13:11-18 ·
THE PROPHETIC UNMASKING OF
THE IMPERIAL CULT

Whereas the author elaborates the moral appearance and bizarre characteristics of the first monster from the sea, he only briefly mentions that the second monster has horns like a lamb but speaks like a dragon. The monster's horns, the symbols of power, are compared to those of a lamb; but the monster's general appearance is not compared in this way. In the present context the reference to the horns and speech of the monster is not just to *any* lamb and dragon but clearly to *the* Lamb and *the* Dragon. The second beast, subsequently called the pseudoprophet (16:3; 19:20; 20:10), exercises the power of the Lamb while it preaches the message and speaks the language of the Dragon.

John thus does not so much elaborate the appearance as stress the function of the second beast. The pseudoprophet seeks to persuade the whole world to worship and to prostrate themselves before Satan and his earthly agent, the first monster from the sea. As the Lamb has created the new royal/priestly community for God (5:9-10), so the pseudoprophet seeks to transform the whole world into a cultic community of Satan worshiping the image of the first monster (13:12). He accomplishes this goal in two ways: by working miracles, and making a cultic image of the first monster; and by branding his followers with a mark on their forehead or right hand.

The first way. Like Elijah, the pseudoprophet works miracles in order to legitimize his activity. The second figure thus functions as the antithesis of the two prophetic witnesses, who also act with the authority and power of Elijah. The visions of the two monsters from the sea and earth therefore seem to express in mythological symbolization the prediction of Mark 13:22 that "false Christs and false prophets will arise and show signs and wonders. . . ." Revelation, however, reinterprets this traditional Christian end-time expectation in political terms.

The pseudoprophet acts as an agent for cultic propaganda by making an imperial image or statue that can speak. It was a commonplace belief in antiquity that cultic images or statues could talk or even move and that the priests of various cults could animate the images of their gods. Although miraculous signs are not directly associated with the imperial cult, the two miracles of the land beast—a cultic image that moves and speaks as well as causes lightning and fiery signs (13:13-15)—are attested to as staged cultic wonders. We have sufficient evidence that rather sophisticated technology was available in the first century C.E. both for producing divine images that could speak, sweat, move, and prophesy and for fashioning devices that could simulate thunder and lightning.

For instance, in his work *Alexander the False Prophet,* Lucian describes Alexander's use of liturgical technology for making a cultic image speak and give oracles:

> As he wished to astonish the crowd still more, he promised to produce the God talking-delivering oracles in person without a prophet. It was no difficult matter for him to fashion crane's wind pipes together and pass them through the head, which he had so fashioned as to be life-like. Then he answered the question through someone else, who spoke into the tube from the outside, so that the voice issued from his canvas Asclepius. (*Alex.* 26)

The second miraculous sign of the land-beast, fire from heaven, probably refers to the use of fiery lightening signs in cultic settings. Thunder and lightning, the symbols of Jupiter's authority and divinity, had been appropriated by Roman rulers. Plutarch (*Moralia,* 780F), for instance, was critical of emperors who imitated divine actions of creating thunder and lightening or emitting sunbeams. According to Suetonius, Octavian's father saw his son in a dream with the thunderbolt, scepter, and insignia of Jupiter wearing a radiating crown (*Aug.* 94.6). Martial refers numerous times to Domitian as well as to Jupiter as the thunderer. Thus it is likely that Rev 13:13-15 alludes to actual practices in imperial cult celebrations of the East.

In Revelation, the cultic image not only has a miraculous impact but it serves to identify publicly the true worshipers of the beast. As those who did not worship the image of Nebuchadnezzar were threatened with death (Dan 3:5-7), so here all those who do not worship the monster's image risk persecution and death (Rev 13:15). This feature of the narrative probably refers to the imperial inaugural cults. Citizens of the empire and especially the provinces expressed their loyalty toward Rome by prostrating before an imperial cultic statue and by burning incense in honor of the divine emperor.

The title "pseudoprophet" characterizing the second beast as well as the reference to the cultic images of idols may also refer readers to the seven messages. These messages speak of Christian prophets who like Paul might have argued that idols are nothing and that therefore Christians are free to participate in the imperial cult. In contrast to the message of these Christian leaders, whom he calls pseudoprophets, John's rhetorical symbolization stresses that behind the cult of the emperor stands Satan. In short, the activity of the second monster may allude to both the imperial cult functionaries and to Christian prophets whom the author opposes.

The second way. The mark on the foreheads and right hands of the beast's followers (cf. 14:9, 11; 16:2; 19:20; 20:4) functions as a counterimage to the sealing of the 144,000. It also characterizes the worshipers of the beast as the rivals of the Lamb's followers. At the same time, the mark on the right hand appears to refer to the currency necessary for any economic transaction. Since the coins of the province Asia had the image of the emperor or of the goddess Roma imprinted upon them, this reference could be another allusion to the imperial cult. Such an interpretation is supported by the fact that Jewish freedom fighters, such as the Zealots, rejected the use of Roman coins. Bar Kochba, for instance, had his own Jewish currency minted because the official coinage bore the imprint of the imperial cult. The economic impact of the beast's mark is underscored in 13:17.

John explicitly interprets the number of the beast. The meaning of the number 666 must have been well known to Revelation's original audience, but it is no longer known to us. In fact, the solution of the mystery was already lost to Irenaeus in the second century C.E. Puzzling out this number is challenging because in John's time the letters of the alphabet had numbers as their equivalent and could therefore be transcribed in a numerical way (e.g., $a = 1$; $b = 2$). This was done for Greek, Hebrew, and Latin. It was easy to transcribe letters into numbers but almost impossible to reverse the procedure if the meaning was not already known, since many possible words might add up to a given number.

Scholars have suggested that 666 is either the numerical equivalent of the title "Nero Caesar" in Hebrew, an abbreviated form of the full name of Domitian, or simply the intensification of the number six, which signifies incompleteness and evil. Since the author stresses that the number stands for a human figure, however, it is not likely that the number 666 has only a generic significance. Whatever the exact meaning of the number 666, its economic value and impact are obvious. As the vision of the first monster ends with the announcement of captivity and execution, so the vision of the second monster ends with the threat of the economic devastation of all those who do not prostrate themselves in worship before the first beast.

The great tribulation of the end time is thus reinterpreted here in political-economic terms. The economic and political oppression and persecution of Christians, as well as of all those who refuse to give homage to the imperial cult, have their deepest roots in the demonic anger of Satan, which fuels the acts of those who destroy the earth. Revelation consistently speaks of the power of Satan in national, political, and cosmic terms (13:7; 18:3, 23; 20:3). Satan deceives the nations and not merely individuals into sinful actions (20:7-8). Revelation's notion of ultimate evil is best understood today as *systemic evil* and *structural sin*.

REVELATION 14:1-5
THE ALTERNATIVE COMMUNITY

This rhetorical section consists of a vision and audition (vv. 1-3) which are followed by the author's explicit interpretation (vv. 4-5). The vision pictures the alternative community of the Lamb, whereas the audition recalls the "new song" of 5:8-10.

The number 144,000, as well as the seal on their foreheads, indicates that the followers of the Lamb are the same group of people as those sealed in 7:1-8. Their location is neither the historical Mount Zion nor the heavenly Zion, since 14:2 clearly distinguishes between Zion and heaven. Rather, Zion refers here to an eschatological place of protection and liberation. According to Isa 24:23 and 25:7-10, at the end of time God will be proclaimed king on Mount Zion, death will be destroyed, and God's people will be liberated from their oppression and the slander against them. The prophet Joel also stresses again and again that on the day of the Lord, Mount Zion will be the place of salvation for all those who call on the name of God.

According to Jewish apocalypses, the Messiah will appear on Mount Zion with the elect while the nations gather for eschatological warfare. He will punish the nations, kill the ruler of the last empire, and gather the community of the elect (4 Ezra 13:25-50; 2 Bar. 40:1f; cf. Rev 17:4). Clearly the vision of the Lamb on Mount Zion constitutes the first in a series of judgment visions and announcements that follow. At the same time it also functions to provide a counterimage to the vision of the first monster. This function is underlined through the characterization and the interpretation of the 144,000.

The vision and audition (14:1-3) describe the 144,000 in a threefold way. *First*, the names of God and the Lamb appear on their foreheads. This feature marks the vision rhetorically as the anti-image to that of the beast's worshipers. Like the Jewish high priest and the provincial high priest of the imperial cult, they (144,000) carry God's name on their foreheads. *Second*, the 144,000 alone are capable of learning the new song of the heavenly liturgy which had been mentioned earlier in 5:8ff. But whereas 5:8-10 elaborates the content of the new song, 14:3 focuses on those who can learn it. *Third*, 14:3 stresses that the 144,000 are redeemed from "the earth," which suffers from the eschatological wrath of God. Thus the vision and audition of 14:1-3 probably refer to the eschatological protection of the redeemed, a protection already promised in 7:1 8 and 11:1-2.

The explicit interpretation of the vision in 14:4-5 does not center on the figure of the Lamb or on Mount Zion but on the identity of the 144,000. They are said to be the first fruits of the harvest, the perfect offering and gift for God. They are the true followers of the Lamb because they refuse to participate in "the lie" and deception of the beast. What is difficult to understand is their characterization as not having "soiled themselves with women." A literal meaning of "women" and of the 144,000 as male ascetics is unlikely since Revelation's language does not function as a cipher with a one-to-one meaning. Moreover, such a misogynist stance appears nowhere else in Revelation. Since Philo (*De Cherub* 49–50) uses the grammatically masculine term *virgins* similarly in a metaphorical sense for God's people, male and female, such a metaphorical use has been understood. A metaphorical meaning of the 144,000 is therefore likely. In addition, celibacy is not stressed elsewhere in Revelation. Since in the rhetorical context and sign system of Revelation sexual language is used metaphorically, the phrase "they have not soiled themselves with women" refers to the idolatry of the imperial cult. Moreover, Babylon/Rome, the great courtesan, is said to be "the mother of all harlots" (17:5), "with whom all the kings of the earth have committed fornication" (17:2). The true followers of the Lamb are praised because they have not drunk "from the wine of her fornication." They are members of the community of the Lamb.

In conclusion, 14:1-5 functions rhetorically in two ways within the overall composition of Revelation. The segment depicts the alternative community of the Lamb as living in the midst of the worshipers of the beast. At the same time it serves as the introduction to the succeeding series of eschatological judgment visions. Like the Synoptic apocalypse, these visions picture the last judgment in terms of a world harvest. The true followers of the Lamb are likened *here* to the faultless first-fruit offerings of the earth. They also symbolize the promise that not all humanity will follow those who "destroy the earth."

Revelation 14:6-13
The Announcement of Judgment

The triple announcement of judgment in 14:6-13 points forward to the series of bowl visions that follow. These bowl visions have as their fulcrum the symbolic narration of the judgment over Babylon. At the same time 14:6-13 refers to chapters 12–13 which have elaborated the alternatives of worshiping the beast or remaining loyal to God and the Lamb. Words of salvation introduce and conclude this threefold announcement of judgment.

The angel flying in midheaven has a similar function to the eagle of 8:13 who announced the three woes. As a complement to the woes, the message of the three angels brings "good news." The first angel calls all humanity to conversion by using expressions of early Christian missionary preaching (cf. 1 Thess 1:9f and Acts 14:15ff; 17:24ff). According to the Synoptic apocalypse, the Gospel had to be preached to all the nations before the end would come (Mark 13:10; Matt 24:14). This expectation is shared by Revelation. The gospel message of the book consists of the call to worship the Creator, the living God. It invites everyone to acknowledge the ultimate source of all life.

The second angel announces with traditional prophetic words (cf. Isa 24:19; Jer 51:7f; Dan 4:27) that judgment has been executed over Babylon. Babylon is first mentioned here. The expression "Babylon the great" recurs in 16:19; 17:5; and 18:2, 10, 21. Most exegetes hold that in the context of Revelation Babylon is a prophetic name for Rome, since Rome was understood in Jewish and early Christian literature of the time as anti-type to Babylon (4 Ezra 3:1-2, 28-31; 2 Bar. 10:1-3; 11:1; 67:7; Sib. Or. 5:143, 159). Both Babylon and Rome shared in the dubious distinction of having destroyed Jerusalem and the temple. Babylon, however, must not be reduced to a simple code or steno-symbol for Rome since John uses the name "Babylon" in order to evoke a whole range of scriptural meanings. Moreover, one can observe here clearly that the symbolic narrative of Revelation does not follow a temporal sequence since the fall of Babylon/Rome will not be narrated until chapters 17–18.

In comparison with that of the second angel, the proclamation of the third angel is considerably more elaborate. One may not, however, construe the punishment of the beast's worshipers as an accurate description or a literal prediction of their fate. Rather, it functions as a prophetic threat and rhetorical exhortation which is expressed in symbolic language. This prophetic threat does not invite Christians to gloat over the torture of their enemies. Instead it calls for steadfast resistance and loyal endurance. In 112 C.E., the emperor Trajan wrote to Pliny, the governor of Bithynia (a province in Asia Minor), that he should punish Christians only if they were accused and convicted. Those who deny "that they are Christians, and make the fact plain by their actions [that is, by worshiping Roman gods] shall obtain pardon." In contrast, the threat of eternal punishment made in Revelation warns Christians and non-Christians alike not to worship idols and not to participate in the imperial cult.

The message of the three angels concludes with a beatitude pronounced by a "voice from heaven." It is underlined in addition by the command to "write down." Just as Paul assures his communities that the dead in Christ will share in the resurrection (1 Thess 4:16; 1 Cor 15:17f), so Revelation assures its audience that Christians who have died can rest in peace because their life-work will vouch for them at the last judgment (20:12f) God will not forget the life, work, and labor of Christians who have died but will reward their deeds.

Revelation 14:14-20
The Eschatological Harvest

The harvest theme links this vision with 14:1-5 which has characterized the followers of the Lamb as the "first fruits," as an offering without blemish. It also corresponds to the expectations of the Synoptic apocalypse (Mark 13:27; Matt 24:30), and the parables of God's reign (Mark 4:29; Matt 13:39). Revelation expands this early Christian eschatological expectation insofar as the text follows the pattern of Joel 3:13 by paralleling the harvest image (14:14-16) with that of the vintage (14:17-20). Although some scholars have suggested that both of these images have the same meaning, this is not likely. Rather, the grain harvest appears to convey a positive message whereas that of the grape harvest symbolizes the wrath of God.

The image of the One in Human Likeness sitting on a white cloud alludes to Daniel 7:13. It clearly marks the figure as identical with the figure of the parousia Christ in Rev 1:7 and 19:11. This figure, preceded and followed by three angels, occupies the center of chapter 14. According to traditional Christian expectation, at the day of God, Christ will send out angels to gather the elect from the ends of the earth (Mark 13:27). In Rev 14:14-16, the harvest image does not, however, simply announce the ingathering of the elect, since 14:1-3 has already symbolically pictured the gathering of the elect around Christ. Rather, it speaks of all the nations, those who accept "the eternal gospel" (14:6-7) and who will worship God (15:3-4).

The image of the vintage (14:17-20) proves more difficult to understand. Some argue that this image conveys the same positive meaning as the harvest image because the vine traditionally symbolized both Israel and the church (Isa 5:1-7; Jer 2:21; Ezek 19:10-14; John 15:1-7). Others argue that since Christ died "outside the city," this was the proper place for the martyrdom of those who held onto the testimony of Jesus (Heb 13:11-13). However, the reference to the "winepress of the wrath of God" which points forward to Rev 19:15 speaks against such a positive interpretation of the vintage image. This text clearly states that Christ will tread the "winepress of the fury of the wrath" of God, the Almighty; therefore, the vintage image in Rev 14:14-20 is most likely influenced by Isa 63:3-6, the picture of Yahweh's terrible vengeance. In Revelation, not Yahweh but an angel executes this terrible carnage. The size of the bloodbath is 1,600 stadia which equals about 180 miles, roughly the length of Palestine. Symbolically the number 1,600 stadia covers the whole world insofar as sixteen hundred is the square of ten (the number of totality) multiplied by the square of four (signifying the four corners of the world). The bloodbath and terror of God's judgment affects the whole world. As I have argued before, however, John's doomsday rhetoric would be misunderstood if it were seen as predictive description rather than as an evocative warning.

Revelation 15:1
The Third Portent in the Sky

Revelation 15:1 introduces the visions of the angels pouring out seven bowls, or goblets. The introduction characterizes this septet of visions as the antipode to the first great portent in the sky, the woman with the child who appears in cosmic splendor. Moreover, the whole series climaxes in the seventh bowl signifying the destruction of Babylon, which chapters 17–18 greatly elaborate and develop.

Revelation 15:2-4
The Eschatological Praise of God's Justice

The praise of the eschatological victors constitutes the fulcrum of the small scroll visions in 10:1—14:20. At the same time, this hymn serves as an interlude to the bowl visions and thereby interprets prophetically the visionary narration of God's wrath. The theological motif of Israel's exodus as the liberation from the oppressive power of Egypt has been woven by John like a red thread into the preceding visions. In 15:2-4 it is made explicit. It also determines the plague visions that follow.

In this climactic vision concluding the little prophetic scroll, John has tied together key images and symbols of previous passages into an impressive rhetorical symbolization of hope. The contrast with the preceding vision of judgment could not be greater! The image of the "lake of glass" refers to 4:6; the "fire" alludes to the wrath of God in 8:5; the "harps" remind us of the "new song" in 5:8 and 14:2; the use of the appellation "victors" indicates the fulfillment of the promises to the victor at the end of the seven messages. In addition, the "lake of glass" recalls the Exodus plagues of the previous seven-cycle. Finally, the assertion of victory in the war against the beast ties this vision to the preceding chapters.

As the Israelites sang the victory song of liberation after crossing the Red Sea (Exod 15:1ff), so here the conquerors sing a hymn of deliverance in praise of God's justice. Almost every word of this hymn can be traced to the Hebrew Bible (cf. Deut 32:4; Pss 86:8ff; 111:2; Amos 4:13; Mic 1:11; Pss 11:2; 139:14). The most influential text, however, seems to be Exodus 15:1-8. The Song of Moses has become in Revelation the Song of the Lamb, the "new song." Both songs praise God's redemptive activity in the deliverance and liberation of the people of God. In addition, the hymn functions also as a positive response to the eternal gospel because it announces that God's justice will cause the nations of the earth to come and worship God. Here, like Caesar, God is called king of the nations. The new song of Revelation announces liberation and salvation not only for the Christian community, but also for all nations which are now oppressed and longing for the experience of God's justice. God's judgments are just and true. Like the chorus in a Greek drama, this hymn interprets the meaning and intention of the preceding and following visions of cruel judgment. Their goal is justice and salvation.

C'. Exodus from the Oppression of Babylon/Rome
Revelation 15:5—19:10

Introduction

This section has already been introduced by the angelic announcements in 14:6-13, and it was opened by the presentation of the bowl angels in 15:1 as well as the hymnic interlude of deliverance in 15:2-4. It is more difficult to decide where the section ends, since the Babylon visions are clearly marked structurally as a part of the last bowl vision; but they serve at the same time as the first part of the literary inclusions: 17:1—19:10 (*a*), 19:11—21:8 (*b*), and 21:9—22:10 (*a'*). Here again one must remember that John does not think in terms of sections or divisions but intends to interlace discrete segments and to join different parts of the composition with each other. The Babylon visions thus form a *joint* that interconnects the two series of eschatological judgment visions with each other and at the same time points to the portrayal of the outcome of God's judgment in the New Jerusalem visions.

Revelation 15:5—16:21
The Seven Bowls of God's Wrath

The seven bowl series of judgments parallels and intensifies the rhetorical symbolization of the trumpet series. While the trumpet plagues have destroyed only one-third of the earth, the bowl plagues bring about its total devastation. The people's reaction to the bowl plagues resembles that which was evoked by the trumpet plagues. The repeated emphasis on the people's lack of repentance recalls the Egyptian plague pattern which stresses that Pharaoh and his people did not repent. How people react to the bowl plagues reveals their true allegiance insofar as they, like the beast, blaspheme the living God.

The bowl sequence also repeats the trumpet pattern in that the first four plagues are visited upon the earth, sea, inland waters, and the heavenly bodies, while the last three afflict the demonic powers of the underworld. But whereas the effects of the four trumpets prove to be general and incidental to people, the bowl punishments are directed specifically against the community of the beast worshipers. Although this focus indicates that *materially* the bowl series functions differently from the trumpet series, it also shows that *structurally* both plague series have the same function. They do not speak of different eschatological events but recapitulate each other and symbolically illuminate different dimensions of the "Great Day of the Lord."

Like the trumpet series, the bowl plagues come forth from the heavenly temple. The expression "Tent of the Testimony" refers to Israel's sojourn in the wilderness and recalls the climax of the trumpet plagues in 11:19. The introduction of 15:1 is restated and elaborated, for the narrative depicts seven angels in the vestments of the Jewish high priest. It also symbolizes the seven plagues with the image of golden bowls. The symbol of the "golden bowl" alludes to the golden bowls of incense mentioned in 5:8, which are explicitly identified as the prayers of the saints.

The smoke filling the temple and the sounds of theophany further recall the introductory vision of the seven trumpets (8:2-5) where the smoke of incense symbolized the prayers of the saints. Fueled by the fire from the altar, there is an explosion of the terrible sounds of theophany. Thus the seven golden bowls filled with the wrath of God seem to announce in symbolic language the same early Christian conviction which 2 Thess 1:6 expresses in plain language: "God will very rightly repay with injury those who are injuring you. . . ." The bowl plagues, therefore, are best understood as representing the heavenly response to the prayers and outcries of Christians for justice. They also seek to warn Christians and non-Christians alike not to become members of the imperial cult community.

The followers of the beast and its universal community become the objects of God's wrath. This is explicitly stated in the narration of the first bowl's effects on those who have the mark of the beast and worship its image (16:2). Both the destruction of Babylon/Rome in the climactic seventh bowl narrative account and the concentration of the fifth bowl plague on the throne of the beast also announce symbolically God's wrath. Yet, the bowl plagues do not bring about repentance as the acts of the two prophetic witnesses did (11:13). Rather, they make public the true nature of followers of the beast who blaspheme God.

The sixth and seventh bowls announce the destruction of Babylon/Rome, which will be further elaborated in the narrative of chapters 17–18. The sixth bowl shows the advance of the enemy kings of the east (Rev 16:12) who will lay siege to Babylon/Rome (17:15-18), whereas the seventh bowl confirms the fall of Babylon that was earlier announced in 14:8 and will be lamented in chapter 18. Rev 16:13-16 is not a part of the sixth bowl narrative, since the kings from the east must be distinguished from the kings of the earth assembled for the great battle on the Last Day; therefore, 16:13-16 is best understood as an interlude which functions as the *formal* equivalent to the interludes before the seventh seal (chap. 7) and the seventh trumpet (chaps. 10–11).

The three evil spirits looking like frogs are the functionaries of the demonic trinity: dragon, beast, and pseudoprophet (16:13-16). They assemble their army for the final battle at a mythological place called Har-Megiddon in Hebrew (i.e., Mount of Megiddo). Just as the meaning of the number 666, so the intended meaning of this name has eluded all scholarly attempts to arrive at an accurate interpretation. The multivalence of the author's mythological-symbolic language cannot be reduced to a single one-dimensional definition! Such multivalence expresses the author's interest in giving prophetic interpretation rather than geographic-eschatological information. Rhetorically, 16:13-16 announces the great eschatological battle, a motif that will be more fully developed in Revelation 19:11—20:10.

The interjection of a traditional Christian prophetic warning in v. 15 indicates how this mythological symbolization of the Day of the Lord should be understood. Revelation's impressive images and mythological narration of the eschatological end time and judgment should not lead readers or hearers to speculation and calculation. Rather, Christ will come like a thief in the night (cf. 1 Thess 5:2ff; Matt 24:42ff; 2 Pet 3:10; Rev 3:3); therefore, one must always be prepared. The judgment rhetoric of Revelation's symbolization aims at engendering an ethic of consistent resistance. Revelation's mythological symbolization of the eschatological wrath of God, however, does not just serve prophetic exhortation but also seeks to give rhetorical assurance and encouragement. Deviating from the plague pattern of the trumpets, John inserts after the third bowl plague a twofold acclamation in order to interpret theologically the whole plague series. The angel of the waters and the altar in 16:4-7 (cf. 6:9; 8:3-5; 9:13; 14:18) praises God's justice and faithful execution of judgment, echoing the Song of Moses and the Lamb in 15:2-4. God's justice will prevail.

Such justice is inflicted neither from the outside nor with despotic arbitrariness. Justice is not an alien imposition by some external authority. Rather, justice is understood as the conviction that each act brings about consequences which must be faced responsibly. It is God who has the power to make sure that all people have to bear the consequences of their actions. All receive what is their due. The Greek text does not speak of punishments but about judgment and justice. Not the desire to inflict punitive torments but the values of equity and vindication motivate and direct God's wrath and judgment.

Revelation 17:1—19:10
The Trial and Execution
of Babylon for Murder

Revelation 16:17-21 connects the seven bowl series with chapters 17–18 in such a way that the outpouring of the seventh bowl encompasses the two chapters that follow. At the same time it completes the series of bowl plagues which began in 16:1. Moreover, one of the bowl angels functions as *angelus interpres* in 17:1. The narrative sequence 17:1—19:10 may be compared to a triptych with three panels. After a general introductory headline in 17:1-2, the first panel (17:3-18) describes and interprets the world capital, Babylon. The second panel (18:1-24) differs stylistically insofar as the destruction of the great city is not described but only reflected in the dirges of the kings, merchants, and shipowners. The legal claim of the persecuted victims against Babylon is now granted. The powerful capital of the world is destroyed not just because it has persecuted Christians but also because it has unlawfully killed many other people. Rev 18:24 must therefore be understood as the theological key to the whole Babylon series of judgments. The third panel (19:9-10) presents a heavenly liturgy praising the justice of God's judgments and announcing the marriage feast of the Lamb.

The whole narrative sequence ratifies the announcement of Babylon/Rome's judgment in 14:8. It both ratifies and gives a more elaborate close-up of the seventh bowl plague. At the same time, the female figure of Babylon/Rome functions as the counterpoint image to the heavenly woman clothed with the sun in chapter 12. It also provides the contrasting image to the bride of the Lamb, the New Jerusalem. Structurally the visions of Babylon are the climax of the third great "portent in heaven." They are, moreover, introduced by the same angel of the bowl seven-series who also shows John the New Jerusalem.

John thus uses the image of woman to symbolize the present murderous reality of the imperial world power as well as the life-nurturing reality of the renewed world of God. It must not be overlooked, however, that such female imagery for cities utilizes conventional language because then, as today, cities and countries were grammatically construed as feminine. In addition, centuries before Revelation, the Hebrew prophets had employed the image of the bride, the wife, or the harlot either for characterizing Jerusalem and Israel or for depicting other nations and their capitals. The female imagery of Revelation, therefore, would be completely misconstrued if it were understood as referring to the actual behavior of individual women. On the contrary, here more than in other sections, Revelation relies on the prophetic language of the Hebrew Bible, which was by then conventional for its gendered imagery and language. Just as, for example, the image of the Lamb refers to an actual historical person and not to animals, so the images of the heavenly woman, the bride, or the harlot symbolize cities as the places of human culture and political institutions and do not tell us anything about the author's understanding of actual women.

REVELATION 17:1-18
THE COSMOPOLIS BABYLON/ROME
AND ITS POWER

Like a headline, 17:1-2 summarizes the content of the whole triptych that portrays the sentencing of and the judgment against Babylon. The metaphor of the "many waters" (v. 15) characterizes Babylon as an international city and as the powerful capital of the whole world. The image of the city as "the great harlot" probably derives from Isa 23:17, which, especially in its Greek form, understands the international commerce and wealth of Tyre as the "hire" paid to a harlot. The statement that "the kings of the earth have committed fornication with her" must be read metaphorically to mean that Babylon has usurped and perverted the political power of all its provinces. The corruption and violence of Babylon/Rome affect all the inhabitants of the world.

After a new introduction, John describes Babylon/Rome in its great splendor. The interpretation following the introduction first focuses on the beast before it sketches the desolation of Babylon. This interpretation climaxes in the explicit explanation: It is the great city that has the ruling power over the kings of the earth. John is then carried "in spirit" to the desert, probably because he sees Babylon being made into a desert (v. 16) according to the decree of God.

Like a goddess, Babylon rides the beast, which has many blasphemous names written upon it. The splendor and wealth of Babylon dazzle even John (17:6-7). Just as the followers of the Lamb have a name written on their foreheads, so too does Babylon. The expression "name of mystery" may allude to the great Mother Goddess. Babylon holds in her hands a golden cup filled with idolatry and detestable things. The content of the cup is explicitly interpreted as the blood of murdered Christians which has intoxicated the great city.

Revelation 17:7-18 gives a lengthy explanation of the beast on whom the woman rides. Like the number 666 in 13:18, this explanation has received much attention since it seems to indicate the period in which the author is writing. The seven heads of the beast are said to be the seven hills on which the woman sits. This location of Babylon appears to identify the world capital as Rome with its seven hills. The hills in turn represent seven kings, of whom five have fallen in the past, one exists in the present, and another is still to come in the future (although, when he comes, he will remain only a little while). The beast in turn represents the eighth king, but it also is one of the seven.

Two possible approaches to the riddle are proposed. One interpretation suggests that this explanation should be understood in symbolic rather than allegorical terms. The seven emperors constitute a symbolic unit of seven but are not to be seen as actual emperors. Just as at the point of the sixth bowl and the sixth trumpet the demonic forces develop the greatest power, so do they here also at the time of the sixth emperor. John locates himself at this point in time in order to let his readers know not only that they live at the height of the destruction perpetrated by imperial power, but also that God's judgment of this power is imminent. As the beast usurps the divine attributes of God (17:8), so it assumes here the number six. As the eighth king, the beast is the antifigure of Jesus—the Antichrist. It is the Antichrist because the number of Jesus was 888 (the numerical equivalent of the name *Iēsous* in Greek is: $I = 10$; $ē = 8$; $s = 200$; $o = 70$; $u = 400$; $s = 200$).

The other proposal for solving the riddle offers a more likely solution that is, however, also far from being conclusive. This second proposal insists that the seven heads of the beast represent actual Roman emperors. No agreement exists, however, as to who should be counted as the first emperor in the series. Since the author must have known that a seventh king would come, some argue that he most probably had Trajan as the seventh king in mind, because Trajan was designated emperor shortly before Nerva's death. Nerva then would have been the sixth emperor in the series. This would date the writing of Revelation to 97–98 C.E., shortly after the murder of Domitian. The Greek word for "they have fallen" speaks of the preceding emperors as having suffered violent deaths. These emperors are Caesar, Caligula, Nero, and Domitian. This solution of the riddle approximates the traditional date of Revelation, which, according to Irenaeus, was written toward the end of the reign of Domitian (81–96).

The enigmatic information that the beast was one of the seven, others argue, may allude to the legend that Nero would return or be resurrected. With the help of the Parthians he would avenge himself and destroy Rome. This expectation seems to be expressed in the figure of the ten kings who will give their power to the beast and destroy the great city. The ten kings cannot be identical with the kings of the earth, since these are said to have given their power to Babylon. Rather, they seem to represent the same entities as the evil army called together by the three demonic frogs, as well as the army of "Gog and Magog" in 20:7ff. They will make war against the messianic king, the Lamb, whose followers are presented in 14:1-5 and 20:4-6, but the Lamb will overcome them (19:11ff). The explanation given in 17:7-18 thus seems to suggest that Babylon represents Rome on different levels: the city, the empire, and the goddess Roma.

Because of John's harsh indictment and criticism of Babylon/Rome, exegetes tend to downplay the political implications of John's vision since it appears to contradict other New Testament writings that have a more positive attitude toward the Roman state (cf. Rom 13:1-7; 1 Pet 2:13-14; 1 Tim 2:1-2). The figure of Babylon the Great becomes, however, depoliticized if it is interpreted as the symbol of the archetypal enmity against God or the sign for the general decadence of all civilization. The Babylon vision is also depoliticized if it is read as calling for an appreciation of the transience of life or as a symbol of the fleeting character of wealth and power. Instead, Rome in its splendor, being carried and supported by the beast, must be understood as the magnificent symbol of imperial power and religion. As such, Babylon is the powerful personification of international oppression and murder throughout the Roman empire. Rome is envisioned as intoxicated with the blood not only of the saints, but also of all those slaughtered on earth. Rome exhibits enormous wealth and holds universal power. Its decrees are carried out in the provinces that support Roman idolatry and instigate persecution of Christians.

REVELATION 18:1-24
PROPHETIC PROCLAMATION OF
ROME'S JUDGMENT

The magnificent picture of Rome flaunting its wealth and power shifts to a scene of doom. The vision of a great angel in heavenly splendor precedes the announcement of Babylon's fall (18:1-3) and the double prophetic oracle of Revelation 18:4-5, 6-8. The series of dirges and lamentations over Babylon (18:9-19) climax in a prophetic call of praise that at the same time has the rhetorical function of pointing to the concluding hymns in 19:1-8. The whole chapter ends with a prophetic sign-action and a summary statement of Rome's indictment: Its crime was murder (18:21-23, 24).

Chapter 18 not only constitutes the middle panel within the overall triptych of 17:1—19:10. It also is composed like a triptych within a triptych. Two proclamations of judgment (18:1-8 and 21-24) frame the series of dirges (18:9-19) that, in turn, are again composed in a tripartite fashion. The kings' lament (18:9-10) and that of the shipowners (18:17-19) frame the central lament of the merchants (18:11-16). The whole sequence forms an artful literary composition whose nestling technique could be compared to a Russian doll containing several other dolls. John achieves a strong unitary composition with imaginative power, although he derives the language and imagery of this section almost verbatim from very divergent sources. His artistic skill proves itself in the interweaving of various, often contradictory, traditions into a unified composition with great rhetorical power.

The splendor, wealth, and might of Rome and the justice of God's judgments define the central images and theological motifs of this section. The whole scene could be likened to a universal courtroom, in which a class-action suit takes place. Plaintiffs in this suit are Christians together with all those killed on earth (18:24); the defendant is Babylon/Rome, who is charged with murder in the interest of power and idolatry; and the presiding judge is God. As announced previously in 14:8, Babylon/Rome has lost this lawsuit and therefore its associates break out in lamentation and mourning, while the heavenly court and the Christians rejoice over the justice they have received. In pronouncing the sentence against Rome, the judge has acknowledged their legal complaints and claims to justice. This sentence is to be executed by the beast and the ten horns, the divine henchmen. Verse 20, therefore, is best translated: "God has exacted justice from her on the basis of your legal claims." To interpret such legal mythologization either as an expression of the author's hate for civilization or as a sign of life's transience would mean to seriously misunderstand Revelation's theology of justice.

A heavenly voice and not John is the narrator in 18:1-20. The heavenly voice begins to speak with the imperative "Move out" in 18:4 and ends with the summons to rejoice in 18:20. Those calls to exodus and rejoicing frame the two narrative sections announcing judgment over Babylon: the judgment oracle and its explanation in 18:5-8 as well as the citation of three funeral dirges in 18:9-19, which make extensive use of the oracles against Tyre in Ezek 26:1—28:19. Three groups of speakers—kings, merchants, seafarers—proclaim their woes over Babylon's fall. Although Rev 18:9-19 is a large-scale reference to Ezekiel 26–28, John does not repeat the order of Ezekiel but follows a different, four-part literary pattern which is repeated in all three dirges: (1) introduction and identification of speakers—kings, merchants, seafarers; (2) dirge against the Great City (Rev 18:10, 16, 19; cf. Ezek 16:23); (3) reference to what is lost in Babylon's destruction; and (4) closing reference to the suddenness of Babylon's fall.

The lament of Rome's associates indicates the sociopolitical location of Revelation. Close economic and political ties between Rome and the provinces, as well as international commerce in the Roman world-state, fostered the growth of wealth not only in Rome but also in the provinces. Historians of antiquity point out that never before had people known the same measure of stability and prosperity as in the Roman Empire of the first century. Only the provincial elite and the Italian immigrants, however, especially the ship-owners and merchants, were reaping the wealth of the empire's prosperity in Asia Minor, whereas a heavy burden of taxation impoverished the great majority of the provincial population. Thus a relatively small minority of the Asian cities benefited from the international commerce of the Roman Empire while the masses of the urban population mostly lived in dire poverty or slavery (18:13).

The author of Revelation sides with the poor and oppressed majority. He not only sharply criticizes the community of Laodicea, which boasts of its riches, but he also repeatedly announces judgment and destruction for the world's rich and powerful (6:12-17; 17:4; 18:3, 15-19, 23). Conversely, the two communities of Smyrna and Philadelphia, which are poor and lacking in power, receive no prophetic censure. Although the first temple of the goddess Roma was erected in Smyrna already in 195 B.C.E., Pergamum became the center of the imperial cult in Asia Minor. As such it also became the religious and political center of the *Koinon*, the organization of the cities of Asia. At the temple of Roma and Augustus in Pergamum the *Koinon* assembled annually for the celebration of games in honor of Roma and Augustus. Although religious in character, the assembly of the Asian cities came to play an important political role in imperial administration.

When the kings and cities of the Hellenistic world lost or gave their power to Rome, they also relinquished to the goddess Roma or to the Roman emperor the honor and cult previously paid to their local gods by Greek or Asian cities. Economic exploitation and retaliation are two of the beast's most powerful weapons for persuading people to participate in the imperial cult. Rome's political domination was thus sustained and augmented by the imperial religion which Revelation indicts as the idolatry of the nations.

Revelation's rhetoric of prophetic exhortation and hope becomes explicit in the twofold oracle (18:4-8) and in the call for rejoicing (18:20). The oracle and the call to rejoice pronounce the sentence on Babylon and confirm that God has made sure that justice is done. The exhortation "come out of her, my people," in turn invokes again the Exodus motif. Just as the Hebrew Bible can refer to the exodus from Sodom, Egypt, or Babylon (Jer 50:8; 51:6, 45), so this call encourages the people of God to leave the "Great City" that in 11:8 has been called Sodom and Egypt. Since the figure of Babylon represents not only the city of Rome but the whole of the Roman Empire, the call to "come out of it" must be understood metaphorically as a call to separate from Rome's injustice, idolatry, and murder. This call has a rhetorical function similar to the sealing of the 144,000 in chapter 7 and to the measuring of the true worshipers in 11:1-2. In the midst of tribulation, it calls for the eschatological exodus of those who have remained faithful until the great day of judgment.

Revelation's theological rhetoric in chapters 17–18 would be misunderstood if it were construed as primarily interested in revenge and the reversal of Rome's fate because its author resents culture, civilization, and city life. Rather, Revelation's symbolic narrative must be read as attempting to engender the hope and encouragement of those who struggle for economic survival and freedom from persecution and murder.

REVELATION 19:1-10
THE SALVATION OF GOD'S REIGN

This whole section climaxes in a double audition. Its content and compositional functions match those of the interludes and hymns in 7:9-17; 11:15-19; 12:10-12; and 15:2-4. At the same time, its content parallels and anticipates the vision in 21:1—22:5. While the antiphony of the heavenly choir (19:1-4) proclaims God's justice and judgment on earth, the major motif of the preceding chapters, the second hymn of the great multitude on earth (19:5-8) expresses joy over the advent of the Lamb's marriage feast, thereby announcing the major motif of the following chapters. Both hymns are molded together through the threefold repetition of "Hallelujah." The whole narrative sequence concludes with a beatitude as well as a dialogue between the angel and the seer (19:9-10).

The three hallelujahs of heaven and earth rhetorically respond to the call to praise in 18:20 and also correspond to the three dirges over Babylon. The expression "Hallelujah" derives from the Hebrew words *halal* and *Yah* (Praise Yahweh) and alludes to the psalms of the Passover liturgy celebrating the Exodus from Egypt (Pss 113–18). Three choirs sing the antiphony of praise: the heavenly multitude (vv. 1-3); the twenty-four elders joined by the four living creatures, who are mentioned here for the last time in Revelation (v. 4); and the great multitude of people on earth (vv. 5-8). Like the "new song" in 5:8-14, the threefold hallelujah is rendered by heaven and earth.

The heavenly choir again asserts the justice of God's judgment over Babylon, whose crime was the murder of the Christian witnesses and the destruction of the earth. The affirmation that God's sentences of judgment are "true and righteous" alludes to the cry of the altar in 16:7, to the announcement of judgment in 11:18, and to the Song of Moses and the Lamb in 15:3. It insists that salvation, glory, and power belong to God. As I have argued before, in Revelation these terms may not be understood in a spiritualized way as though they are referring just to the individual soul. Rather, both terms together must be interpreted in their political context and meaning.

The Roman emperor Augustus, for instance, was called "savior of the Greeks and of the whole inhabited world," "savior and benefactor," "savior and founder," and "savior and god." His birthday marked the beginning of "good tidings" (gospels). He was regarded as the "just and generous lord" whose reign sustained peace and happiness, that is, salvation. By utilizing these terms, the heavenly choir asserts: It is not the power of Caesar but God's power and salvation that is revealed in the justice meted out to Babylon/Rome and to its vassals and provinces. Whereas Rome's colonialist rule spells domination, submission, robbery, plunder, and slaughter (see Tacitus, *Agricola* 30), God's power and salvation call for jubilation, feasting, and well-being.

The hymn of the great multitude on earth (19:5-8) reminds readers of the eschatological multitude in 7:9ff, and it recalls the new song that the Lamb's followers sing on Mount Zion (14:2ff). The singers here, however, include not just Christians, the servants of God, but all those who have responded to the call of the gospel proclaimed by the angel in 14:6. Those who fear God, the small and the great, participate in the praise of God's reign over the earth (v. 5). God's reign spells salvation and not oppression. It can be likened to a great wedding feast, for the myth of divine marriage was widespread in antiquity; and the Hebrew prophets had long ago adopted this myth to express the relationships between God and Israel. The wedding feast as the image of eschatological salvation was also well known from early Christian tradition (Matt 22:3-14; Luke 14:16ff; cf. Matt 26:29 and Luke 13:29).

The image of the church as the bride of Christ appears especially in the Pauline tradition (Rom 7:2-4; 2 Cor 11:2f; Eph 5:25ff). In Revelation, however, the bride represents not the church but the New Jerusalem (21:2, 9), the renewed world of God. The "righteous deeds" of Christians give splendor and glory to God's envisioned world. Not all Christians who were originally invited to the wedding feast, but only those who have faithfully responded to this invitation through their righteous life-praxis, will be blessed. They will participate in eschatological well-being symbolized by the marriage feast (Matt 22:11-14). Like the three previous beatitudes or blessings, the fourth blessing functions rhetorically as a warning and as a promise. The author's authentication, "these are the true words of God," refers not just to this beatitude but to the whole section of Rev 17:1—19:8 and to the content of the book itself.

The concluding scene in v. 10 stresses two major themes of Revelation: First, the angel is on the same level as the prophet because both have the same function, namely, to proclaim the "witness of Jesus." The interpreting angel of apocalyptic literature here is engaged for and at the same time subordinated to Christian prophecy. Second, no one, except God and the Lamb, may receive the cultic prostration of obeisance demanded by the imperial cult. To prostrate oneself (the Greek word *proskynein* is usually translated as "worship") before an angel or before the imperial image would mean to acknowledge and give obeisance to their authority, power, and kingship, an acknowledgment due only to God. Therefore, Revelation's call to worship would be misconstrued if it were merely understood in a spiritualized, liturgical, or pietistic sense. If the author would write today, he might say: "Don't salute the flag, salute God"; or "Don't pledge allegiance to the state, pledge it to God."

Although the prophetic rhetoric of Revelation is replete with cultic language and imagery, its social location and theological goal are not liturgical but political. Worship and praise in Revelation serve political ends and ethical decisions. John's prophetic-apocalyptic rhetoric employs conventional cultic vocabulary (such as temple, altar, priest, items of clothing, incense, libation bowls, and lamp stands), liturgical settings, doxological formulas, hymnic compositions, and hieratic scriptural language not for the sake of persuading his audience to participate in the daily or weekly liturgy. Rather, he utilizes such cultic language derived from Israelite and Greco-Roman cultic practices for the sake of moving the audience to political resistance. He seeks to motivate them either to give obeisance to the power and empire of God and the Lamb or to the dominion of Babylon/Rome. True, John intends his book to be read and heard in the assembly of the Christian community, and Revelation's cultic language and imagery have greatly influenced subsequent Christian rituals and liturgical practices. Nevertheless, John's liturgical rhetoric does not seek to inculcate religious-cultic practices. Rather, it functions to interpret the symbolic-apocalyptic narrative of Revelation, which seeks to give prophetic interpretation and exhortation of the religious-political situation in which Christians find themselves at the end of the first century C.E.

**B'. Liberation from Evil and
God's World-City
Revelation 19:11—22:9**

Introduction

The final visionary sequence of Revelation takes again the literary form of an inclusion and intercalation. As shown previously, the visions of 17:1—19:10 constitute the development and climax of the last plague septet. At the same time they make up the first panel (*a*) in the triptych 17:1—22:9 because they are a part of the "last judgment" scenes (19:11—21:8) depicted in the central section of the triptych (*b*). The destruction of the evil forces is thus presented in reverse order from that of their introduction. Babylon/Rome, although mentioned last, is judged first. This judgment precedes the punishment of the antichristic/imperial powers by the parousia Christ (19:11-20). The following series of the last judgments climaxes in the punishment of the dragon/Satan (20:1-10) and in the destruction of the powers of the underworld (Hades). The universal judgment of all the dead (20:11-14) inaugurates the appearance of God's renewed creation and the well-being of God's people (21:1-8).

Babylon/Rome, the antichristic imperial forces, and finally the dragon/Satan are overcome and punished. The last enemies to be judged are the powers of Death and Hades. God's intended world is a world without any oppressive and dehumanizing powers. God's judgment spells salvation for the earth and for all those who have not cooperated with evil, destruction, and murder. The last panel of this triptych and the climax of the whole book presents the New City of God as the anti-image of Babylon and of Satan's reign (21:9—22:9'). The visions of the New Jerusalem further depict and develop the motif of eschatological salvation announced in the hymnic praise of 19:1-10.

Revelation 19:11—21:8
Parousia and Final Judgment

The parousia-vision of Christ ushers in the visions about the day of final judgment. The symbolic rhetoric of the three judgment visions of 19:11-21 (especially vv. 11, 17, 19) promises that the two beasts will be punished with eternal torment and that their followers will suffer death. Three additional judgment visions (20:1, 4, 11) present the punishment of Satan, the reward of faithful Christians, and the general judgment of the world. These three visions complete the "last judgment" visionary series that culminates in the vision of eternal life with God (21:1-8). This vision constitutes the formal interlinking *joint* to the sequence of the New Jerusalem visions.

The interpretations of these visions vary widely. The vision of the "thousand-year reign," the so-called millennium, has especially received much scholarly attention. Yet it must be kept in mind that the "last judgment" visions speak about "events" or "truths" beyond space and time. One would misunderstand this visionary series, therefore, if one would view it as presenting a chronological sequence or a description of future events rather than as a mythological symbolization of eschatological salvation. In these visions, John employs traditional mythological language and symbols for narrating the "end" and the "beyond" of history. The series provides a spectrum of related images that express final salvation following upon the last judgment. The sequence of these visions does not seek to convey chronological information. Rather, its approach is topical, describing in various ways ultimate salvation in its different aspects.

REVELATION 19:11-21
THE CONFRONTATION BETWEEN CHRIST
AND ANTICHRIST

The threefold "and I saw" (19:11, 17, 19) divides this segment of Revelation into three visions: the appearance of the parousia Christ (19:11-16); the gory counterimage to the marriage feast of the Lamb (19:17-18); and finally, the punishments of the two beasts and the death of their followers (19:19-21). It appears that at the conclusion of this series of punishments no human being remains alive.

The following aspects seem crucial for understanding the rhetorical aims of this passage:

The first aspect. Exegetes generally agree that the vision in 19:11-16 speaks of the eschatological return, the parousia, of Christ. Although the identity of the victor on the white horse is not explicitly stated, his description repeats features of the introductory section of Revelation (cf. 1:5, 14, 16; 3:7, 14) and thus clearly identifies the figure as Christ. But whereas the seven message series in the beginning of Revelation had depicted Christ as the judge of the Christian community (1:20), 19:11ff presents him as the judge of the nations. Christ is the ultimate antagonist of the imperial and demonic forces. The parousia Christ appears as a mighty warrior followed by his heavenly army; however, no battle is recorded.

Christ receives the title of "Great King" because he manifests his rule over the nations (19:15). Just as the dragon and beast had worn diadems signifying their universal dominion, so Christ wears many diadems characterizing him as ruler of the world (19:12). This divine warrior-king comes to execute judgment (19:12). Although John stresses that no one except Christ himself knows his own name, the text nevertheless alludes to several titles beginning with the title "Faithful and True" who judges with justice (cf. 16:5-7; 19:2). This title stresses that Christ's punishment is just and refers simultaneously to Rev 3:14, which calls Christ the "faithful and true witness." The justice meted out by the parousia Christ gives proof of his loyalty and faithfulness toward those who have kept his witness.

No one but Christ himself knows Christ's true name. Since according to folklore the power of persons resides in their name, this secret name (19:12) implies that no one can have power over Christ. The title "The Word of God" seems to suggest Wis 18:15-16 as a source for John's image:

> [D]own from the heavens, from the royal throne, leapt your all-powerful Word; into the heart of a doomed land the stern warrior leapt. Carrying your unambiguous command like a sharp sword, he stood, and filled the universe with death. . . .

The series of christological names climaxes in the title "King of kings and Lord of lords," a variation of the title of the Lamb in 17:14: "Lord of lords and King of kings." Thus the parousia entails the manifestation of Christ's universal rulership.

The second aspect. The gory summons of the birds functions rhetorically as a threat. It is not intended to be a concrete depiction of cruel judgment but rather an urgent warning. The figure of the angel in midheaven refers the audience both to the eagle of 8:13 who had announced the three woes as well as to the angel of 14:16 who had proclaimed the eternal gospel. Here, the hyperbolic announcement of divine punishment repeats the threat of God's and the Lamb's wrath, which has already been proclaimed at the opening of the sixth seal (6:14-17). Although the gory image of the "great supper of God" evokes revulsion, it seems restrained when compared to the scenes of punishment and revenge found in later Christian apocalypses.

The third aspect. The last attempt by the beast and the pseudoprophet to make war recalls the trumpet interlude of 16:13-16, where the three demonic frogs had assembled an army at Armageddon. It must be noted, however, that in chapter 19 the actual eschatological battle is never pictured. John employs the traditional language and imagery of eschatological warfare for forensic rhetorical purposes. The beast and its pseudoprophet, who represent the destructive political power and the imperial cult of Rome, are not killed but taken captive and thrown into a malodorous and fiery lake. It is important to note here that their punishment is different from that of their human followers, who are not thrown into the lake of fire to be tormented but instead are killed instantly.

Revelation 20:1-15
Liberation from Evil and
Universal Judgment

Like the preceding vision, 20:1-10 develops the depiction of the demonic army in a variety of ways. This army has already appeared in the narrative symbolization of the fifth trumpet (9:1-11) and in the rhetoric of the interlude to the bowl visions (16:13-16). As in 16:13, here also the dragon commands the rebellious forces. The elimination of these powers and their subsequent punishment proceeds in two steps (20:1-3, 7-10). Although the chapter *formally* divides into three visions, with 20:7-10 as a part of the vision beginning in 20:4ff, *contextually* 20:7-10 brings to conclusion 20:1-3. The vision of the so-called millennium thus functions structurally in two ways: as a part of the second vision, 20:4-10, and also as an interlude within the overall vision describing the punishment of the ultimate forces of evil (20:1-3, 7-

10). In addition, the expressions "first resurrection" and "second death" mark 20:4-6 as a parallel narrative to the vision of judgment in 20:11-15.

The following three observations may help one to understand this difficult text:

The first observation. After the punishment of the two beasts, Revelation recounts the punishment of the dragon in two steps: In a first step, the angel, who resembles the "star" from chapter 9 and holds the key to the abyss, takes the dragon captive, casts him down into the abyss, and seals his prison for a thousand years (20:1-3). The four names of ultimate evil—the dragon, the old serpent, the devil, and Satan—refer the audience to 12:9, where the great dragon together with his angels was cast down to earth. Now the "short while" of his wrath on earth has passed, and he is thrown down into the underworld. In a second step, the dragon, released from his prison in the underworld, gathers a ghost army from the four ends of the earth and marches against the camp of the saints and the "beloved city"; however, as in 19:19-21, no battle ensues. Instead, fire from heaven devours the army of Gog and Magog, and the devil suffers the same fate as the two beasts. Their punishment signals the final and everlasting destruction of all evil and demonic power (20:7-10).

Scholars debate whether the army of the devil consists of living nations or whether it is a universal army of the dead. That the doors to the underworld were thought to be located at the four ends of the earth speaks for the latter interpretation. Moreover, according to 19:17f and 21, all human beings are said to have perished. Finally, the names Gog and Magog are mythical names. They probably are to be understood here as the mythological place-name Armageddon is understood in 16:16. The whole vision thus appears to refer to the same final demonic battle narrated already in 9:1-11; 16:13-16; and 19:19-21. The "events" described in these visions do not take place in time and space but belong to the "beyond" of human history; therefore, they are depicted in very ancient mythological language and imagery.

The second observation. John probably narrates victory and punishment over the dragon in two steps in order to show that even during the eschatological assault of the demonic forces faithful Christians will be protected. This seems to be the reason why he sandwiches the vision of the millennium (the thousand-year reign of Christ and the victorious Christians) between the capture and the final assault of the devil and his army. He also structurally characterizes the millennial vision (20:4-6) and the eschatological assault as one and the same visionary unit. If this is the case, then only the devil's captivity but not the reign of the victorious Christians (22:5) is intended to be limited to a symbolic time span of a thousand years.

In my opinion, the interlude 20:4-6 then has a similar rhetorical function to that of the vision about the sealing of the 144,000 (7:1-8) and the injunction to measure the temple of the true worshipers (11:1-2). It aims to assure the audience of the protection and salvation of the elect. But whereas the preceding interludes have referred to Christians still living during the end time, this vision shows how those Christians are rewarded who have been killed because of their witness. The vision of the millennium thus functions as a parallel to the vision of 6:9-12. Now, the number of those who have still to die according to 6:9-12 is complete. The end is here!

The vision of 20:4-6 promises that those who were killed because they had refused to pledge allegiance to the imperial cult will receive justice. The "souls" of those Christians who were executed "come to life again" and assume rulership together with Christ. The phrase "come to life again" does not connote in Revelation a spiritual or a limited resurrection since it refers in 2:8 to the resurrection of Christ and in 13:14 to that of the beast's heads (cf. Matt 9:18; Rom 14:9). Rather, this vision of the millennium speaks about the final resurrection of those Christians who have died in their resistance to the imperial cult and have remained loyal to God and the Lamb. Because they have ratified their baptism with their life-praxis (1:6; 5:10), they assume their eschatological reign as priests.

John employs here the Jewish expectation of a messianic kingdom, which was by then probably traditional, in order to stress the reward of those Christians who have "overcome." The concluding beatitude underlines this literary function of the vision in 20:4-6 by stressing that those who participate in the "first resurrection" are exempt from final judgment and eternal punishment. As priests they share in the life-giving ruling power of God and Christ. They are the "camp of the saints" protected from the last assault of all demonic and evil powers.

The third observation. The image of the great white throne in the universal judgment scene of 20:11-15 parallels the throne image in 20:4 and recalls the throne room of chapters 4–5. Before the throne stand all the dead of the whole world and of all of history. Every human being has the right to receive a just sentence from the divine Judge. It seems that John imagines ledgers wherein the recorded deeds and life-praxis of the dead appear. These ledgers are distinguished from the "book of life" in which the names of those found "not guilty" are recorded. Only those found guilty are thrown into the lake of fire. This is what is probably meant by the expression "second death," which the faithful need not fear.

Finally, the "last enemy" (cf. 1 Cor 15:26), Death, along with its abode, Hades, meets destruction. The present earth and heaven corrupted by evil, life-destroying forces vanish away in order to make room for a world and creation as they are intended by God. Although John has retained the apoca-

lyptic tradition of a last judgment, he has radically altered traditional understandings of a limited, preliminary messianic kingdom in order to produce a
vision of reward for those faithful unto death. He uses apocalyptic traditions
about a messianic interim kingdom (cf. 4 Ezra 7:26-33; 2 Bar. 29–30) in
order to stress that those who have died in their struggle with the oppressive
power, Babylon/Rome, will be exempt from the general judgment and rule
forever with Christ.

REVELATION 21:1-8
THE LIBERATED WORLD OF GOD

The series of messianic judgments in Revelation reaches its fulcrum in the
vision of a qualitatively new and different world. This vision functions simultaneously as an introduction to and as an exposition of the following visionary
section depicting the New Jerusalem (21:1 is taken up in 22:1-5; 21:2 in
21:9-11; 21:3 in 21:22f and 22:3; 21:4 in 22:2; 21:6 in 22:1; 21:7 in
22:4; 21:8 in 21:26f and 22:3). After the visions of a qualitatively new
world and of the New Jerusalem (21:1-2) follows a proclamation alluding to
the Exodus motif (21:3-4). The vision of God's "different" world of salvation
is ratified by God-self with a promise to the victor and a stern warning to
those who are tempted by the ways of the dragon and the pseudoprophet beast
(21:5-8). The conclusion of this visionary unit thus indicates once again that
one may not construe Revelation as predictive description but instead must
understand it as prophetic encouragement and persuasive exhortation.

The "first" heaven and earth now belong to the past, since they were determined by the antagonistic dualism between the reign of God and Christ in
heaven and that of the dragon and his allies on earth and in the underworld.
The "new heaven and earth" stand in continuity with the former heaven and
earth, but they form a qualitatively new and unified world. This new reality
is characterized by God's presence among the peoples of God. The vision of
the New Jerusalem, arrayed like a bride in the splendor of the "righteous
deeds of the saints," makes symbolically present God's eschatological salvation and reign which require that heaven will move down to earth.

Christians who have been persecuted and embattled because they have been
both the claimants of God's empire on earth and opponents of the empire of
Babylon/Rome are now victorious. Unlike Paul, John does not envision that
at the Last Day Christians "shall be caught up" in the clouds to meet their
Lord (1 Thess 4:17), nor does he hope, as Daniel did, that the righteous shall
shine like stars in heaven (Dan 12:3f). Rather, the center of the theological
vision and rhetorical movement of Revelation is the earth. This new earth
differs from the earth as we know it, in that "heaven will be on earth."

Revelation's vision of salvation centers on the earth. Christ's and God's rule
and power cannot coexist with the dehumanizing power that corrupt and devastate the earth (19:2). The outcries of the persecuted for the enactment of

justice and judgment therefore also rise up on behalf of the earth as God's creation. God's justice and judgment bring not only vindication of those persecuted and murdered but also engender total human well-being and salvation on earth. Not suffering, weeping, mourning, hunger, captivity, and death, but rather life, light, and happiness determine the reality of the new heaven and earth (cf. 7:9-15); therefore, the sea, the place of the beasts and the symbol of evil (13:1), no longer exists (21:1). The future intended world of God's salvation is not envisioned as an island but as encompassing all of creation.

An explicit word of God ratifies this vision, identifying eschatological salvation as the nonoppressive, liberating presence of God, whose name is Emmanuel, that is, "God with us." As in 1:8, so here too God's name is "Alpha and Omega." It is God who makes everything new. This vision of eschatological salvation clearly has rhetorical functions since it concludes with a promise and a warning. Those who will remain victorious will be the heirs of God's liberated world (cf. the promises to the victor in chaps. 2–3). Those who participate in the destructive praxis of the antidivine, oppressive powers will suffer the second death of eternal punishment.

Again the catalog of evildoers in 21:7-8 (cf. 22:15) is not comprehensive or descriptive but exhortative. It highlights the various ways of participating in the treason against God's empire. The cowards lose courage in the struggle with the antidivine forces; the faithless and polluted become the followers of Babylon; the murderers become the beast's agents in killing those who resist its might; the fornicators, sorcerers, and idolaters worship the dominion that destroys the earth; and finally, the liars commit themselves to the fundamental and ultimate falsity that breeds violence. These vices do not represent abstract lists of generalized moral failures but, rather, exhort the audience not to betray God's world and intention of well-being and salvation.

Revelation 21:9—22:9
The City of God

This last series of visions magnificently elaborates the visionary symbolization of eschatological salvation in 21:1-8. It is structurally designed to form the third panel in the triptych 17:1—22:9, because, like the Babylon visions, it is introduced by one of the seven bowl angels (cf. 21:9; 17:1) and concludes with a dialogue between the angel and the seer (cf. 22:6-9; 19:9-10). In contrast with 17:1 where John is carried into the wilderness, in 21:10 he is carried to a great mountain where one of the bowl angels shows him the "bride, the wife of the Lamb" (21:9). Just as Babylon/Rome (17:1), the great harlot or courtesan, is arrayed in scarlet and purple and adorned with gold, jewels, and pearls (17:4, 16-17), so the New Jerusalem sparkles with precious jewels and pearls (21:18-21). It radiates from the glory of God like jasper, a most rare and precious gem, clear as crystal (21:11). Nothing unclean and no abomination scars the beauty of the New Jerusalem (21:27; 22:3a) in contrast with the gaudy appearance of Babylon, which is called "the mother of abominations" (17:5). Just as the harlot has a name written on her forehead (17:5), so the citizens of the New Jerusalem have "God's name on their foreheads" (22:4). Their own names are written in the "Lamb's book of life" (21:27) in contrast to Babylon's followers, whose names are "not written in the book of life" (17:8). Whereas the "kings of the earth" not only become vassals of Babylon/Rome but in the end also destroy it (17:15-18), the "kings of the earth" bring their glory to the New Jerusalem (21:24).

In short, John depicts the eternal glory of the New Jerusalem as the dwelling place of God (21:10—22:5) by contrasting it with Babylon's doom as the dwelling place of demons (18:1-3, 9-19). Through these compositional parallels and contrasts John draws the picture of the New Jerusalem as the anti-image of the great city Babylon/Rome. He contrasts the splendor and power of the Roman Empire with that of the empire of God and Christ in order to encourage readers to resist the murderous power of Rome. This series of visions embroiders the fulfillment of the promises given to the victorious at the end of the seven messages.

In the introductory verses to this vision, John again stresses that the New Jerusalem comes down from heaven containing within it the glory of God. After describing the city in all its splendor (21:11-14), he details its measurements (21:15-21) and depicts its paradiselike life (21:22—22:3). The whole section climaxes in the vision of the eternal reign of God's high-priestly servants (22:4-5).

Like the visions of chapter 20, the New Jerusalem vision derives its materials from Ezekiel 37–48. John, however, does not only expand the material taken over from Ezekiel 40ff with features from Isa 54:11-17; 61:1-22; 62:1-12; but he is aware of a whole range of apocalyptic traditions about the New Jerusalem (Zech 12:1—13:6; Tob 14:4-7; 4 Ezra 8:52; 10:2-7; 44:54-55; Ap. Dan. 5:4-13; 1 Enoch 85–90; Sib. Or. 3:552-731; 5:361-433). In addition, he also seems to model his depiction of the New Jerusalem after the historical city Babylon, known to us from the Greek historiographer Herodotus, insofar as he says that the city stands "foursquare" and gives its size in furlongs, measurements that are found in Herodotus's text. It is therefore possible that Revelation's audience may have recognized that John's visionary description of the New Jerusalem alludes to that of the historic Babylon and thereby pictures God's city as the anti-image of Babylon.

John, however, molds features taken over from traditional materials and sources in such a way that they express his own vision of future salvation and well-being. First, he elaborates not only on the size but also on the overall description of the wall surrounding the New Jerusalem, a feature which receives only scant attention in Ezekiel. Second, John does not describe the temple but the city, whereas Ezekiel focuses his narrative on the new temple. Third, John stresses that the throne of God and the Lamb are the center of the New Jerusalem. Fourth, John appeals to Greco-Roman hopes to live in the ideal city. Thus the overall vision of the city of God gathers the preceding theological motifs and the various visions of eschatological salvation together into a final focal vision.

The first feature. The city and the wall around it are clearly distinguished. Whereas the city seems to function as the universal cosmic symbolization of salvation, the wall appears to represent symbolically the Christian community. On its twelve gates are chiseled the names of the twelve tribes of Israel (7:1-8). Moreover, the wall rests on foundation stones bearing the names of the twelve apostles of Christ. These foundation stones resemble those precious stones which adorned the breastplate of the Jewish high priest. In such a way, the wall of the city becomes a symbol of the eschatological Israel, the high-priestly people of God (22:4f), the church founded, according to Christian tradition, upon the twelve apostles (cf. Eph 2:20). It must not be overlooked, however, that it is not the city itself but only the wall surrounding it that symbolizes the eschatological community of the church.

Observing the distinction between wall and city helps one to understand the curious measurements with which the seer describes their relationship. An enormous discrepancy exists between the size of the city and the size of the wall. Whereas the size of the city measures approximately 1,200 miles, that of the wall measures about 144 feet. This enormous difference in proportion indicates that the universal cosmic salvation of the world by far exceeds that figured in the Christian community. These cosmic universal dimensions of the new city of God are intermingled with paradisiacal features of the new creation. Not only faithful Christians will share in the glory, splendor, and life eternal of the New Jerusalem, but all those whose names were registered in the book of life at the final judgment on the basis of their works.

The second feature. While the visions of Ezekiel center on the description of the new temple, Revelation states flatly that no temple will be found in the city of God. At first glance, this statement seems to run counter to Jewish eschatological hopes which John generally cherishes. It must not be forgotten, however, that the whole city has the form of a perfect cube and as such is characterized as the Holy of Holies (cf. 21:3). The sacred symbol of the temple has now given way to the reality of God's presence here on earth.

The "servants of God" can therefore be pictured as high priests who have the name of God engraved on their foreheads. But whereas the Jewish high priest had the privilege of entering the Holy of Holies (1 Kgs 6:20) only once a year, the eschatological "high priests" will be in the presence of God forever. Like Moses they will see God face-to-face (22:4f). According to 1:6 and 5:10, Christians were appointed priests for God at their baptism. By referring the audience to these texts, Rev 22:4f promises that those who ratify their redemption with their life-praxis will exercise their priestly right to live in the presence of God (cf. 7:15f).

The third feature. The center of the new city of God is the throne of God, the symbol of imperial power and sovereignty. Yet, not only the Christian community but now all the nations will be the peoples of God (21:3; cf. 15:3). Just as the world-city Babylon/Rome represented the Roman Empire gathering in its precincts the political power and commercial wealth of the nations and their rulers, so too the New Jerusalem will contain the nations' power and splendor. But whereas Babylon/Rome misused its power and wealth for destroying and corrupting the earth, the eschatological vision of God's universal empire promises new life, health, and happiness. The throne—the symbol of God's power from which all judgments are issued—becomes now the source of eternal life and happiness (22:1-3).

Within this universal empire of God, symbolized by the image of the New Jerusalem, Christians who have remained faithful will reign forever (22:5). The promises of 3:21 and 5:10 are now fulfilled. Nothing will endanger their participatory reign and sovereignty (20:4-6). This empire and power of God, of Christ, and of the victorious, however, is not oppressive and dehumanizing, but rather full of life, light, wealth, health, and eternity. Although Rev 2:27 had promised that those who will be victorious will share in Christ's ruling power over the nations, Revelation never pictures any serfs and subjects of this reign. Not oppressive rulership and subordination but the life-giving and life-sustaining power of God characterizes God's eschatological reign and empire.

The fourth feature. John's narrative symbolization of the eschatological city of God, the New Jerusalem, evokes a range of rich meanings that appealed not only to Jewish imagination but also to Greco-Roman desires. The symbolization of the eschatological city reflects much of the Hellenistic hope for the ideal city. It also alludes to Rome's proud claim to be the "Eternal City," a claim found on coins and descriptions of John's time.

Like Hellenistic cities, the New Jerusalem does not have a temple area as its center, but a broad main street for procession, commerce, and public discourse. Its citizens have the power of ruling, but this rule is not domination over others but the power of self-determination. Their life is sacred like that of priests. God's ideal city is not only a universal and inclusive city with a population drawn from all nations, but it is also magnificent and beautiful, radiating with gold and pearls, the treasures of kings and nations. Life in God's city is free of injustice and vice, curse, and the evil powers of the "sea." Tears, crying, pain, sorrow, hunger, thirst, death are no longer found in it. Although there are still "insiders and outsiders," the gates of God's city are permanently open.

Revelation imagines God's final salvation as a world in which nature and culture are integrated. The New Jerusalem also fulfills Roman idyllic as well as Jewish apocalyptic hopes for the "golden age" and "paradise." Through the center of the city flows the "river of life." The leaves of the "tree of life" have the power to heal the nations. In short, the narrative symbolization of God's eschatological city integrates heaven and earth, city and nations, culture and nature, sacred and profane, Israel (twelve tribes) and Christianity (twelve apostles), bride and harlot, Babylon/Rome and Jerusalem, center and boundary. Revelation's final visions imagine heaven as world, world as city, and the New City as open inclusive place of citizenship and well-being for all.

A'. Epilogue and Epistolary Frame
Revelation 22:10-21

The last verses of Revelation appear to be, at first glance, a collection of very loosely related sayings which create a disjointed impression. Yet, insofar as vv. 8-9 clearly parallel 19:10, they are the proper conclusion of the third panel which was introduced in 21:9. The emphatic expression "I John" refers the hearer to the prologue at the beginning of the whole book. Insofar as Rev 22:6-9 both elaborates on 21:5b-8 and also refers to 1:1ff; 3:14; and 19:9b, it appears to form a compositional *joint* that interlinks this epilogue with the last series of visions.

Interpreters generally assume that the one who speaks in v. 6 ("and he said to me") is the bowl angel who has shown John the New Jerusalem; however, in 22:7, the speaker is clearly Christ himself. It is more likely, therefore, that in 22:6, as well as in 22:10f, the speaker is also Christ rather than the bowl angel. If this is the case, then 22:6-20 contains a series of revelatory sayings and oracles pronounced by the Resurrected One. Only 22:8f, 17, 21 are not attributed to Christ.

Structurally, Revelation 22:21 forms the conclusion to the open pastoral letter which was introduced in 1:4f. Just as the epistolary introduction has alluded to the traditional Pauline letter form, so too does the conclusion, which resembles 1 Cor 16:22-24. After a conditional formula of sacral law introduced with "if anyone . . . " (cf. 1 Cor 16:22 and Rev 22:18f), an anathema or curse follows. The curse in turn is followed by the prayer-call "Marana tha" (1 Cor 16:22; Did. 10:6), that is, "come Lord Jesus," which was a part of the eucharistic liturgy. Just as 1 Cor 16:23f concludes with a wish of grace, so too does Rev 22:21.

Contextually, the epilogue seems to serve three purposes:

The first purpose. It hammers home the message that the time until the end is very short and that the Lord will return very soon. This motif of imminent expectation is repeated here four times (vv. 6, 7b, 12, 20), but it occurs only three times in the rest of the book (1:1; 2:16; 3:11). Because of this stress on imminent expectation, John receives instruction not to seal the book (v. 10), in contrast with Daniel, who is told to seal up the words of his prophecy "until the time of the end" (Dan 12:4). These expressions of imminent expectation in Revelation, however, focus not on the day of judgment but on the eschatological coming of Christ, who is here imaged in Davidic messianic terms (v. 16; cf. 5:5; Num 24:17). Christ also is compared with the "morning star," the star of Venus and the sign of sovereignty and victory over the nations. Like God (cf. 1:8; 21:3), Christ is the beginning and the end (cf. 1:17; 2:8). The Spirit, the Bride, and those who hear the words of prophecy respond to the announcement of Christ's imminent parousia with the outcry and prayer: "Come, come Lord Jesus."

The second purpose. The epilogue underscores that the book's intention is rhetorical. It does not give historical and eschatological information or future predictions, but, rather, provides prophetic exhortation and motivation. Two of Revelation's seven beatitudes are found in this section (22:7; cf. 1:3; 22:14; cf. 7:14; 16:15). The list of vices found in 21:8 is repeated almost verbatim in 22:15, and a prophetic oracle of impenitence and righteousness (22:10f) is pronounced. At the same time, it is emphasized that Christ, who will come speedily, will reward everyone according to their life-work (22:12; cf. 20:13; Rom 2:6; 1 Pet 1:17). The urgency of Revelation's imminent expectation clearly serves rhetorical functions.

The third purpose. The final purpose of this lengthy epilogue is to give prophetic authentication. John stresses again and again that it is Christ who witnesses and guarantees the content of his prophecy (22:16, 18). John therefore concludes his book with a solemn declaration of blessing and curse (22:18f; cf. Deut 4:1ff). Although this solemn declaration seems to reflect liturgical and apocalyptic theological convention of the time, it nevertheless indicates that John found it necessary to secure the authority of his prophecy (1:3; 22:6, 9-10, 18-19) by claiming a fourfold inspiration: God, Christ, the Spirit(s), and the apocalyptic angel of revelation (cf. 1:1-3; 22:6; 8f, 16, 18) authorize the book of Revelation.

PART THREE

THEO-ETHICAL RHETORIC

In the preceding commentary section I have incorporated rhetorical analysis with hermeneutical practice. My interpretation of the text has utilized rhetorical lenses for understanding the meaning of Revelation as a historical discourse. Attempting to do justice to its historical-theological vision, I have attempted to show that Revelation's text is best understood as a rhetorical practice concerned with issues of power, values, and commitment. In contradistinction to other early Christian writings, Revelation presents a deeply political theo-ethical world of vision. Its central theological concern is not apocalyptic speculation on the course of history or the provision of an exact schedule for the end-time events. Rather, Revelation's central problem and topic is the issue of power and justice.

Such a hermeneutical reading of Revelation's visionary rhetoric strives to recreate its *first* textual meaning and its sociohistorical contextualizations. Such a hermeneutical interpretation would be misconstrued, however, if it were understood as the repetition of Revelation's "first meaning." It does not present an unequivocal transcript of what the text meant so that a practical theological application can translate it into what the text means for today and render it effective for our own time. Rather than as a repetition of the original text, exegetical commentary must be understood as a rhetorical practice that seeks to present a coherent interpretation of Revelation. Reading a text always entails making sense out of it. In doing so, one seeks to attend to all the elements of a text but inevitably privileges some and neglects others. In order to assess the historical-theological adequacy of such a hermeneutical reading and the visions and values it places in the foreground, one must contextualize it within the broad range of interpretations offered by scholarly and public discourses on Revelation.

In this last section of the book, therefore, I will reflect on my own interpretation of Revelation as such a perspectival reading. I do so in order to contribute to the development of a contextualized, praxis-oriented model of biblical interpretation. Such a rhetorical model of theo-ethical praxis approaches Revelation and its interpretation as a discursive site of competing voices and struggles. By recontextualizing biblical interpretation within present-day discursive practices, such a theo-ethical rhetoric seeks to enable and compel readers to reflect on their own practices of reading. It seeks to make connections between the sociopolitical locations and religious-ideological assumptions that color a theological reading of a canonical book such as Revelation. Such a praxis-oriented model of reading does not attempt to provide clear-cut answers but interpretive lenses that invite us to comprehend the interactions between our own readings of Revelation and the sociopolitical and religious locations which shape these readings. At the same time, such a praxis-oriented rhetoric remains aware that our theo-ethical imagination is being molded and formed by biblical texts and their traditions. A liberationist model of rhetorical practice invites readers of Revelation and other canonical texts to become active and responsible participants in the production and critical assessment of theo-ethical meanings and values.

Rhetorical analysis not only seeks to grasp and reconstruct the communicative interaction between a text and its sociocultural contexts; it also attends to the rhetorical situation that provokes the discursive interaction between a text's author and audience. It attempts to recapture not only the voice of the author but also the other voices which s/he engages and which the discourse of the text submerges or represses. It reconstructs the sociocultural location of a work not merely as a passive scene or static background but, rather, as a structured rhetorical situation to which the text can be understood as an active response. Thus Revelation's world of vision is best understood as a rhetorical response to a particular sociohistorical communicative situation.

In order to understand the text of Revelation and subsequent readings of it as socially situated rhetorical practices, one has to distinguish between the *textual* rhetorical situation (i.e., the ways the text construes the problems and issues at hand) and the *actual* historical-rhetorical situation that has generated Revelation's rhetorical world of vision. The interpretive reconstruction of the *actual* historical-rhetorical situation of an argument, therefore, can not proceed on the basis of its own text only but must utilize all available sources.

A rhetorical situation is characterized by a specific *exigence,* urgency, or gravity that engenders a particular speech act. The given difficulty or crisis of the rhetorical situation determines the mode of discourse to be chosen and the type of change to be effected. Any discourse obtains its persuasive character from the difficulty or crisis of the rhetorical historical situation that generates it. Moreover, a rhetorical situation is not only marked by the exigence that elicits rhetorical discourse. It is also constituted by certain *constraints* which impose limits upon the persuasive power of the author and affect the perception, decision, and action of the audience. Although an interpreter must distinguish between the textual and the actual rhetorical situation, s/he must nevertheless reconstruct both as partially overlapping discourses in order to preserve the suasive power of Revelation as a fitting response to a particular rhetorical situation.

The textual, as well as the actual, rhetorical situation of Revelation's world of vision is also found in other parts of the book but is especially *inscribed* in chapters 1–3. The series of seven prophetic messages in the form of imperial edicts follows roughly the classical rhetorical arrangement. Each begins with a *proem* consisting of the address to the recipient and the introduction of the sender (e.g., 2:1), followed by a *narration*, or statement of facts (e.g., 2:2-3). After this follows the *proposition*, or statement of major points (cf. 2:4-6). Each message ends with an *epilogue* consisting of a warning and a promise to those who conquer (e.g., 2:7) in order to generate the desired effect (*pathos*) on the audience.

The central part of the messages comprises information about the audience and its situation. The rhetorical perspective and interest of the author govern the depiction of the sociotheological location which the seven churches in Asia Minor have in common. In 1:9, John stresses that he shares with the audience a common sociotheological location. He defines this common location as tribulation, *thlipsis* (i.e., pressures and difficulties); empire, *basileia* (i.e., their status in the empire of God or Rome); and as endurance, *hypomonē* (i.e., staying power). The middle term *basileia*, which is usually translated as "kingdom" or "reign," can refer to both the empire of Rome and to the empire of God. In Rev 1:5-6, John addresses the audience as those who were made a *basileia* and priests for God. Although they live in the Roman Empire, they are representatives of God's empire and power here on earth through the redemption of Christ. The exigence of the inscribed rhetorical situation is determined by the tension between their common experience of tribulation and their common empire-status, a tension which calls for consistent resistance or endurance.

A. Rhetorical World of Vision:
Empire

Christians have been liberated and appointed to be the representatives and agents of God's power and empire on earth. Therefore, they are locked into a struggle with Babylon/Rome, whose imperial powers are the agents of the demonic and destructive power of Satan. The "dwellers of the earth," the free and the slaves, the merchants and kings, have each submitted in turn to the imperial world power which corrupts and devastates the land.

As the designated heirs of God's power on earth (1:6; 5:10), Christians are bound to run into conflict with this world-destroying totalitarian empire and its allies. Some have already suffered at the hands of this anti-divine, totalitarian enemy power. Rev 6:9-11 refers to those who have been slaughtered and killed because of their witness to God and Christ. They ask the key rhetorical question of the book: How long, O Sovereign? They voice the centuries-old query of those who suffer injustice and oppression: "When, O God, will you vindicate our faith and restore justice to us?" Revelation's outcries for judgment and justice (6:9; 15:4; 18:20), however, rise up not only on behalf of Christians but also on behalf of the whole earth. Revelation utilizes the conventional traditional *topoi* of the Exodus plagues and of holy war not for the sake of revelling in bloody pictorialization, but in order to elaborate rhetorically drastic visions of judgment. God has the power to reestablish justice and thereby to bring about a qualitatively different cosmopolitan world (21:1-7).

The empire-status of Christians generates Revelation's rhetorical problem as a question of power and justice. Revelation's central theological query is: To whom does the earth belong? Who is the ruler of this world? The book's central theological symbol is therefore the *throne*, signifying either divine and liberating or demonic and death-dealing power.

Christian belief in Jesus Christ not as one of many cultic gods but as the lord of the world, by definition had to run into conflict with the proclamation of Roman civil religion: Caesar is Lord! Revelation maintains that the one who "makes all things new" and the one who is "Lord of lords and King of kings" is one and the same. The final establishment of God's and Christ's empire here on earth brings total salvation not only for Christians but also for all those who are now oppressed and slaughtered by the present political powers. Taking the point of view of those who are poor and have little power, Revelation projects its alternative world of vision and symbolic universe in socioeconomic language and political-mythological imagery. By positing a politically transcendent and eschatological "other world" as the horizon of this world, Revelation's dualism challenges the notion that injustice and oppression are at the center of the universe.

Conversely, Revelation maintains that God's and Christ's judgment brings about the destruction of all those "who corrupt the earth." The power behind the political domination of the imperial world power which "corrupts the earth" is not merely human. It is Satan, the antidivine power par excellence. Whereas the heavens rejoice over the devil's downfall, the earth is in anguish:

> Woe to you, O earth and sea, for the devil has come down to you in great wrath because he knows that his time is short. (12:12)

The dragon-devil has given to the beast from the sea, the Roman emperor, "his power and his throne, and his great authority" (Rev 13:12). This power appears to be absolute and universal. It affects Christians and non-Christians alike:

> Also it [the beast] was allowed to make war on the saints and to conquer them. And authority was given it over every tribe and people and tongue and nation and all who dwell on earth will pay obeisance to it. . . . (13:7f)

God's judgment brings justice to those who have rejected the oppression of the great world power, Babylon (19:12). God's coming brings judgment on those who have usurped God's and Christ's reign over the earth. The eschatological victory hymn in 11:17-18 expresses both aspects of God's coming judgment.

> We give thanks to thee, Lord God Almighty, who art and who wast, that thou hast taken thy great power and begun to reign. The nations raged, but thy wrath came, and the time for the dead to be judged, for rewarding thy servants, the prophets and saints, and those who fear thy name, both small and great, and for destroying the destroyers of the earth.

God's judgment and reign, which are here announced in hymnic praise, are narrated in the symbolizations of the final visions of the book. Babylon, the two beasts, and finally the dragon are overcome and punished. The last enemies to be judged are Hades and Death. The "new" earth is an earth free from all life-destroying and oppressive powers. God's judgment means liberation and salvation for the whole earth and all of humanity. The newness of this eschatological earth and world is thus constituted by the absence of evil and oppression. It is envisioned as an alternative to the present world of suffering, exploitation, and death. God's empire on earth cannot be thought of as coexisting with any dehumanizing power that destroys the earth.

The oppositional dualism between the first heaven and the first earth, as well as the antagonistic dualism between earth and underworld, is overcome. The earth that was caught in the antagonistic dualism between divine and demonic power will become a unified world, a world centered around the "tree of life." John, unlike Paul, does not envision that at the Last Day Christians shall be "caught up together with the dead in the clouds to meet the Lord" (1 Thess 4:17). Rather, he sees the New Jerusalem, the holy city of humanity, "coming down out of heaven from God" (21:2). The boundary between heaven and earth is transformed. The voice from the throne proclaims final salvation on earth:

> Behold, the dwelling of God is with human beings. God will dwell with them and they shall be the people of God. And God-self will be with them; God will wipe every tear from their eyes, and death shall be no more, neither shall there be mourning nor crying, nor pain anymore. For the former things have passed away. (Rev 21:3-4)

In sum, the last section of Revelation pictures the glory, life, light, and happiness of God's empire of salvation, which is open to all the nations and free from all oppressive powers and dehumanizing forces. Revelation's political-mythological world of vision does not "spiritualize" human oppression but instead unmasks and condemns it as against God's intention. Moreover, John's rhetorical world of vision does not know of any metaphysical, ultimate dualism between the power of God and the power of evil. God's dynamic power for life manifests itself in the midst of death and spirals in ever widening circles toward the integrity of an undivided world.

It is important to recognize that Revelation's dualistic worldview is rooted in a socioeconomic political situation of oppression. Revelation's dualism is a limited dualism insofar as the demonic powers generating Roman oppression and its religious legitimizations have only a limited time period of activity. The present time is of critical importance because a cosmic-political struggle has ensued with the death and exaltation of Christ. Revelation seeks to encourage Christians to participate actively in this struggle, the outcome of which is already known. The situation of oppression will be abolished and a qualitatively new earth will be the outcome of this struggle, a world that is free from all dehumanizing oppressive powers. Revelation's world of vision is cosmopolitan and not sectarian.

Such a liberationist reading of Revelation's rhetoric subordinates the book's depiction of cosmic destruction and holy war to its desire for justice, which is repeated throughout the book. It puts in the foreground those rhetorical features of the text that aim at moving the audience to practical engagement in this struggle for God's qualitatively new world of salvation. Readings that, for instance, focus on the destructive powers of the plague visions rather than underline their goal of liberation from Babylon/Rome's oppression, or readings that stress the mythological features of holy war and the outcries for revenge, lead to a quite different perception and theo-ethical evaluation of Revelation's world of vision. Such interpretations that attribute the destruction of the world to God are dangerous at a time in history when nations have the technological means to stage the annihilation of all living beings and to bring about the cosmic cataclysms of atomic annihilation and deadly plagues of biological warfare. In contrast, a liberationist interpretation underscores that in constructing the symbolic universe of Revelation John does not call for the destruction of the earth. Rather, he seeks to persuade the audience to see their present sufferings and hardships as a part of the struggle for God's world, which is free of oppression.

The heavenly liturgies and celestial hymnody of Revelation serve rhetorically to elaborate God's power and empire. They do not have liturgical but political-theological functions. Since Roman political power was ratified in cultic terms, the symbolic universe of Revelation must appropriate cultic-religious symbols in order to draw its audience away from the magnificent symbols and cultic drama of the imperial cult. Yet such an appeal to cultic imagination was difficult, since Christians had no cultic institutions—neither priests, nor sacrifices, nor temples. John, therefore, had to derive his cultic language and symbolism not only from the traditional temple cult of Israel, but also from the cultic celebrations which were popular in Asia Minor.

By taking over traditional Jewish cultic symbols—such as temple, altar priests, sacrifices, vestments, hymns, incense, cultic purity—John attempts to construct a symbolic alternative to the splendor of the imperial cult. In doing so he seeks to appeal especially to Jews and Jewish Christians, who "own" the tradition, in order to persuade them to accept his world of vision. Revelation's appropriation of the cultic symbols and institutions of Israel serves rhetorical purposes. Revelation's cultic symbols do not describe or refer to actual cultic practices of Jews and Christians in Asia Minor, as some scholars have argued, but, rather, utilize cultic symbolism as evocative language.

Revelation's utilization of cultic language is not restricted, however, to the appropriation of Jewish religious symbols. The heavenly liturgy celebrated in the throne room of God (chaps. 4–5) bears striking resemblance not only to the Oriental court ceremonial but also to that of the imperial cult. Just as God is depicted as holding a scroll, so in Roman art the emperor is depicted as surrounded by his council and holding a petition or letter as an open scroll. Moreover, the hymns of Revelation allude to the hymns of praise mentioned in the court ceremonial. Hymnic acclamations and signs of obeisance were not reserved for the emperor but were also paid to his representatives in the provincial celebrations of the imperial cult. In addition, talking and moving divine images as well as fiery light-signs were not unknown in cultic settings and were probably also utilized in the imperial cult. Finally, the visions of the New Jerusalem fulfill the ideals of the Hellenistic cosmopolitan city and the idyllic projections of the Pax Romana.

Revelation's language and imagery for the divine is rooted in Near Eastern court protocol and Roman imperial ceremonial. By likening God's glory and power to Roman imperial power and splendor or in portraying Christ as "divine warrior" and "King of Kings," Revelation is in danger of conceiving divine power in terms of Roman domination as "power over," and as oppressive power. Although the author seeks to transform this language and imagery of kingship and dominion in two ways, it is doubtful whether he succeeds in the minds of many readers today. The promises to the victorious and the announcements of the kingly rule of the faithful in the eschatological future never do mention any objects of such rule. In addition, nurturing and compassionate images of God, such as those found in Rev 7:16-17 and 21:3-4, do function as theological correctives; however, they are not sufficiently strong to determine the image of God and Christ in the overall rhetorical symbolization of the book. Since Revelation is not the only biblical writing that promotes the image of an Almighty-Warrior-King-Father-God, the function of such God-language in a democratic society must be assessed. Insofar as such patriarchal language for God fosters and inculcates patriarchal militarism and oppressive domination, it must be changed. Christian theology and liturgy must replace such divine symbolizations expressed in terms of imperial might and destructive warfare with language and metaphors for God and Christ that foster human creativity, democratic responsibility, and engaged resistance to all political powers that dehumanize, oppress, and destroy.

In short, just as resistance poetry does, Revelation constructs a world of vision that challenges the symbolic discourse of Rome's hegemonic colonizing power. It does so by fashioning a rival symbolic discourse of power and empire that seeks to unmask the force of evil sustaining Rome's dominion in order to alienate its audience from the persuasive power of Rome's hegemonic vision.

Simultaneously, Revelation's symbolic universe and persuasive world of vision seek to motivate the audience to pay obeisance solely to God and not to Roman state, religion, and cult—even if such a decision should threaten their livelihood and well-being. Revelation's world of vision therefore is best understood as a rhetorical response to its political-historical and religious-communicative situation from a particular social location. The author's point of view and rhetorical intent can only come to the fore, however, if one reconstructs the rhetorical situation that has engendered John's world of vision in such a way that Revelation's rhetorical symbolization can be understood as a "fitting" response to it.

B. Rhetorical Exigence:
Tribulation

Revelation's inscribed or textualized rhetorical situation suggests that some Christians of Asia Minor might have suffered deep tensions between their faith and their everyday experience. As Christians, they believed in the ultimate power of God and Christ. At the same time, they experienced daily vulnerability, alienation, harassment, marginality, and suffering. Their everyday experiences ran counter to their belief in God's might and undermined their hope in God's empire, glory, and life-giving power. This tension between their faithful conviction and their negative experience in everyday life must have provoked difficult theological questions: If God and Christ possess ultimate power in the world, why do their loyal followers have to suffer? Why does Christ not return in glory without delay to prevent further suffering and to adjudicate justice? Revelation's rhetorical world of vision can be understood as a fitting response to such or similar theological questions. It is not simply the sociopolitical exigence or the christological vision of faith but the interface and interplay between both that constitute Revelation's "rhetorical situation."

Scholars have generally assumed that Revelation along with other apocalyptic writings is best understood as *crisis literature*. They have reconstructed the rhetorical situation that has engendered the book as one of conflict between Christians and the demands of the imperial cult in Asia Minor. According to Revelation's own testimony, Christians had suffered harassment and even death because of their witness to Jesus. Popular interpretation conjures up images from books and movies such as *Quo vadis?* which picture graphically the debauchery of Rome and the suffering of Christians who are thrown to the lions in public games for pagan entertainment.

This widely held "crisis" interpretation of Revelation, however, has recently been challenged by scholars who point out that we lack evidence of an official widespread persecution of Christians under Domitian. Domitian was not worse than any other emperor preceding or following him. He received his bad press from writers who sought to depict his reign in negative colors in stark contrast to that of Trajan. Since there was no real crisis attributable to persecution, Revelation can no longer be understood as addressing a sociopolitical crisis situation. Scholars have developed different arguments for explaining why the *textualized* rhetorical situation conjures up a situation of crisis although the *actual* sociopolitical situation appears not to have been one of persecution.

The first proposal argues that Revelation addresses a situation of "relative deprivation" that the author has perceived as a crisis situation. Revelation's rhetoric of suffering and martyrdom compels readers to direct their feelings of aggression, enmity, and hate against themselves. By projecting feelings of resentment, aggression, and revenge onto a large cosmic screen, Revelation displaces these longings for revenge upon God and Christ. Just as by means of elaborate fantasies a schizophrenic is able to live with existential pain and terror of reality, so Revelation offers for Asian Christians an escape from reality.

A second interpretation denies that the book addresses any crisis situation at all. Rather, the element of crisis is a commonplace topic in apocalyptic literature. It is due to the choice of the genre "apocalypse" and does not tell us anything about the actual social and political situation in Asia Minor. Exhortations, assurances, warnings, threats, and blessings also are generic elements which point to an apocalyptic point of view but not to sociopolitical circumstances. In short, Revelation arises from normal, ordinary life that does not involve any out-of-the-ordinary situation, spiritual bankruptcy, social upheaval, or political oppression. Rather, in its ordinariness, Revelation is appealing to an audience made up of ordinary people, who more or less share in the provincial prosperity of Asia Minor and whose life was not much different from our own.

A *third* approach insists on a purely theological reading of Revelation. Revelation is not written in response to a sociopolitical rhetorical situation but is written in response to the death and exaltation of Christ. Revelation's devastating portrayal of the world is the result of apocalyptic Christology. It is determined by John's unfaltering commitment to the worship of God and Christ. Because idolatry (i.e., polytheistic religion) characterizes the very fabric of society, culture, and the state, Revelation speaks of God's judgment of the world. John, therefore, stresses that the only appropriate response in heaven and on earth is worship. In the present worship of the church, God's reign is already realized here and now on earth.

These different interpretations are not completely inappropriate to the text, but they stress different aspects and features of it. They must be assessed in terms of the theo-ethical values and visions they engender in their sociopolitical contexts of reading. The objections against understanding Revelation as rooted in a sociotheological crisis situation make a sharp distinction between the textualized rhetorical situation and the actual historical rhetorical situation, between ideal and material reality, between theology/worship and everyday experience, between cognitive faith/worldview and sociopolitical structures. Philosophical, theological, psychological, or sociological idealism, however, reproduces the universalist abstract epistemology of traditional biblical studies that obscures the fact that the Scriptures and their interpretations are always framed by the sociocultural locations and theopolitical commitments of those who engage in such signifying practices.

The insight that Domitian was neither better nor worse than other Roman emperors does not prove that Revelation's world of vision is not developed in response to an actual sociotheological crisis. It only suggests that the author's interpretation was not shared by everyone in the Christian community or in the wider Asian society. Although one's view and interpretation depend on *how* one perceives a particular situation of crisis, it also depends on the social location and conscious stance from *where* one looks at such a situation: for instance, a homeless, black single mother will have experienced American life in the 1980s as much more determined by poverty and violence than a white male politician or middle-class executive who has never encountered hunger and destitution would have experienced it. If she is a black feminist she will be able to interpret and articulate her experience in terms of racism, sexism, and economic exploitation. If one understands the ordinariness of life from the social location and the standpoint either of the poor or of the wealthy, one would come to quite opposing conclusions and evaluations of American life today. The same actual historical situation is experienced and interpreted quite differently depending on the analysis and stance taken by the interpreter.

Although the social relations between the province of Asia and Rome were fairly stable, and life in the cities was generally flourishing, one needs to keep in mind that such an assessment represents the perspective of the powerful and wealthy. Many inhabitants of the cities of Asia Minor, staggering under the colonial injustices of oppressive taxation often combined with ruinous interest rates, were suffering from the widening gap between rich and poor. They were afraid of Roman repression of disturbances, paranoid prohibition of private associations, and suspicious surveillance by neighbors and informants. Whereas the vast majority of the population suffered from colonialist abuses of power, exploitation, slavery, and famine, some citizens in the senatorial province of Asia enjoyed the benefits of Roman commerce and peace as well as the comforts and splendor of urban life and Hellenistic culture. If Revelation stresses the economic exploitation and oppression perpetrated by Babylon/Rome's imperialist power, then it expresses an assessment of life in Asia Minor that was not necessarily shared by all Christians.

It may be true that Christians were not officially persecuted under Domitian or Trajan. This does not mean, however, that the experience of persecution and execution was not real or was completely foreign to Christians. The memory of Nero's persecution in 64 C.E.—whose victims were covered with skins of beasts, torn by dogs, nailed to crosses, or consumed by flames (see Tacitus, *Annals* 15)—must have been still alive in the communities of Asia Minor.

In addition, the correspondence between Pliny, the provincial governor of Asia Minor, and the emperor Trajan at the beginning of the second century testifies to the fact that Christians were denounced and executed in Asia Minor even before Pliny arrived on the scene. He mentions that some had left the Christian group "as many as twenty-five years ago." Those who were denounced as Christians and who then confessed were either immediately tried and executed or sent to Rome if they were Roman citizens. Those who recanted or claimed never to have been Christian had to invoke the gods, sacrifice before statues of the gods and the image of the emperor, and curse Christ (Pliny, *Epistle* 10.96–97). Pliny's letter indicates that the Christian group aroused a fundamental suspicion and uneasiness among Romans and Asians alike. The Christian cult was seen as troublesome, antisocial, and as endangering the sociopolitical fabric of the empire. Apparently minor charges could be construed as treason, and Christians were particularly vulnerable to such charges.

Pliny states in plain words what Revelation expresses with the narrative symbolizations of the beasts and the great harlot. Yet Rev 13:17 adds another aspect when it stresses that those who do not have the mark of the beast cannot buy or sell. Not only threat of harassment, imprisonment, and execution, but also economic deprivation and destitution will have to be suffered by those who refuse to take the mark of the beast. Although exegetes are uncertain how to explain the mark of the beast and its number, its economic significance is plain. The beast as a symbol of Roman imperial-cultic power not only threatens the followers of the Lamb with death, but it also makes it impossible for them to live.

Revelation's visionary symbolization of eschatological salvation and well-being and its denunciation of all destructive powers have throughout Christian history inspired chiliastic movements more than establishment Christianity. Whereas mainline Christianity has often co-opted or neutralized Revelation's political-religious language and vision by identifying God's empire with the institutional church or with the interior salvation of the soul, messianic-prophetic Christian movements have again and again affirmed Revelation's vision of salvation as a vision of total well-being and freedom from oppression. They have read it as promising liberation from oppressive ecclesiastical structures and from the destructive domination of those who have power in this world. They have maintained that the empire of God means salvation for this world and not merely salvation from this world or salvation of the soul. Oppressive powers, whether they be political, social, or religious, cannot co-exist with the life-giving empire and power of God. The outcry of Revelation for justice and judgment can be fully understood only by those who hunger and thirst for justice.

John's attempt to formulate the reality and meaning of eschatological salvation in sociopolitical language gains greater significance again at a time when those who share the author's stance toward sociopolitical oppression and exploitation attempt to formulate their own theology of liberation and to stake their life on it. As we have seen, the Guatemalan poet-in-exile, Julia Esquivel, utilizes in her long narrative poem, "Thanksgiving Day in the United States," the language of Revelation to denounce the United States as Babylonian states whose false prophets "twist the truth calling their intervention into Central America and the Caribbean 'peace and development' in order to silence the outcry of the thousands being crucified in El Salvador and Guatemala" (Esquivel, *Threatened with Resurrection*, 89).

It might very well be that many will feel as helpless or resentful vis-à-vis such a prophetic liberation theological rhetoric as they feel vis-à-vis the theology of Revelation. One will not be able to perceive their vision unless one also shares the theological analysis of those who experience United States' culture, society, and religion as destructive and oppressive. In a similar fashion, the author of Revelation has adopted the "perspective from below" and has expressed the experiences of those who were poor, powerless, and in constant fear of denunciation. Revelation's world of vision responds to the experience and predicament of those Christians who are powerless in terms of the political powers of their times.

Such a plea for the appropriate sociopolitical location of Revelation's theo-ethical rhetoric—and our own—does not mean, however, that one should uncritically adopt its symbolic language and theological "world of vision."

Rather, as a partial theological response in a particular sociohistorical situation, Revelation's narrative symbolization calls for critical assessment and theo-ethical evaluation in a contemporary rhetorical situation. Such a critical evaluation is necessary because the symbolic world of Revelation is not only a theo-ethical model *of* its own sociopolitical world but also a theo-ethical model *for* the sociopolitical and religious life of its readers. The language and metaphors we use generate new insights, move us by their appeal to the senses and imagination, and shape our perception of the world in which we live.

C. Rhetorical Motivation:
Resistance

The symbolic rhetoric of Revelation seeks to deepen the loyalty and commitment of its audience by stressing that Christ is alive although he was killed. Its symbolic discourse aims at engendering staying power by promising that the audience will share in the power and glory of the New Jerusalem if they resist the powers of death which now determine their lives. To those who are poor, harassed, and persecuted, but remain faithful and loyal, God promises the essentials of life for the eschatological future: food, clothing, shelter, urban citizenship, security, honor, power, glory.

Utilizing the conventional languages of myth, example, and custom, the author of Revelation does not engage in esoteric apocalyptic speculation or simply give hortatory injunctions. He neither analyzes the problems of his day nor does he directly discuss them. Rather, like contemporary resistance poetry, Revelation achieves pathos primarily by constructing a "symbolic universe" and "plausibility structure." Although Revelation's world of vision is articulated in cultic language, such language serves to symbolize the struggle between divine and imperial power. Rather than writing a theological sermon on "the last things" or a moral exhortation on how to act, Revelation seeks to move its audience to action with the power of its images and visions. Its rhetoric does not seek to evoke just an intellectual response but also wants to elicit emotional reactions and religious commitment.

Revelation's dynamic rhetoric does not aim at producing quietist spiritualism but seeks to engender prophetic motivation for decision and action. Since the "words of prophecy" are to be proclaimed in the worship assembly of the community, Revelation's rhetorical discourse creates a new plausibility structure and a symbolic universe that unfolds within the rhetorical framework of an open letter. Apocalyptic vision and explicit admonition have the same rhetorical function. Revelation provides the vision of an alternative world in order to motivate the audience and to strengthen their resistance in the face of Babylon/Rome's overwhelming threat to destroy their life and livelihood.

Revelation's persuasive aims are theo-ethical; therefore, no fixed impermeable boundaries are drawn between those who are saved and those who are not, between Christians and non-Christians. As signalled by the first seven-series of the messages at the beginning of the book, judgment begins with the Christian community. Just as the *ekklēsia* of Laodicea is condemned because it says that "I am rich and have grown wealthy, and have need of nothing" (3:17), so the audience is warned not to become too sure of its salvation. Christians still can lose their freedom and salvation by becoming slaves to the earth-destroying power of Babylon/Rome. Thus, Revelation gives great prominence to an ethic of commitment. Such a political ethic and commitment seeks to prevent readers from projecting evil only onto others while holding themselves exempt from it. Revelation proclaims and visualizes judgment against the dehumanizing powers of evil in order to warn readers not to succumb to the very concrete pressures of these powers.

Revelation's rhetorical discourse, therefore, begins and ends with a section of censure and an exhortation to faithfulness. The injunctions, beatitudes, warnings, and promises, which run like a red thread through the book, have the rhetorical function of directing the audience to right action. Revelation's symbolic world of vision in turn seeks to motivate its audience to steadfast resistance by giving courage and hope to all those who follow the Lamb and do not accept the mark of the beast. Revelation's rhetorical discourse elaborates visually the life-threatening destructive forces of the evil power and cult of the colonialist state. Conversely, it highlights in mythological language that God, the creator, and Christ, the liberator, remain the legitimate regents of the world. The "eternal gospel" therefore calls all who dwell on earth to repentance, and it enjoins Christians to loyal resistance against the beast and its pressures. Revelation engages in a radical ethical dualism that places before the audience an either-or decision. Either one succumbs to the oppressive world power of Babylon/Rome and its religious legitimization or one engages in the struggle for God's qualitatively new *cosmopolis* that is free from all oppression and evil.

In order to engage the emotions and desires of readers for such a choice, Revelation's symbolic rhetoric utilizes the sociopolitical symbols of two cosmopolitan cities, Rome and Jerusalem, as representing the opposition between two worlds: one constituted by the powers of oppression, the other by those of liberation and well-being. The powers behind these two cities are portrayed in animal figures, two beasts and the Lamb. The two contrasting city-symbolizations are in turn figured as female (harlot/bride) so that a contrast between two groups of linked images is constituted: Harlot–Beast–Babylon with Bride–Lamb–New Jerusalem.

The female images for both the oppressive and the eschatological redemptive community are conventional and traditional. Cities were conventionally figured as female because, in antiquity as today, the grammatical gender of "cities" and "countries" was feminine. More importantly, John derives the image of the bride of the Lamb as well as that of the harlot or courtesan,

Babylon, from prophetic tradition. The image of the marriage of Yahweh with Israel (cf. Hos 2:19; Isa 54:5-6; Ezek 16:8) originally might have been drawn from the sacred marriage-myth that was a typical element of the combat-myth pattern. This image is applied in other early Christian writings to the relationship between Christ and the church (Eph 5:21-33).

Revelation's theo-ethical persuasion employs prophetic invectives when speaking of idolatry as "fornication" and as "defilement with women." John also draws from classic prophetic literature the repertory for the lurid depiction of the harlot-city. The metaphor of the harlot and of "sexual misconduct" derives especially from Ezekiel 16 and 23 but is also found in other prophetic writings. In the prophetic literature, sexual imagery and metaphors of sexual misconduct generally refer to the people of Israel or to its city, Jerusalem. It is frequently used by Hosea, Ezekiel, and other literary prophets to speak about Israel's idolatry and syncretistic practices. The emergence of such a sexual objectification of women and the employment of the metaphoric language of sexual misconduct for idolatry comes close to what feminist analysis terms "sexual pornography." Its emergence in classical prophecy can be seen as related to social and psychological disruption caused by political events.

John did not invent but took over from tradition the symbolic contrast harlot/bride for portraying the opposition between the world of Rome and the world of God. This prophetic symbolization, however, which was by then traditional, does not only obscure Revelation's political interests but also deflects the audience's decision and motivation for religious-political resistance. These traditional sexual metaphors do not draw the audience into a process of decision against Rome's political oppression and its religious legitimization. Rather, they shift attention from Revelation's rhetorical emphasis on justice and focus instead on gender polarity. Readers displace the call to political resistance against evil by construing it in dualistic-moralistic terms of gender and sexuality. The alternative between the empire of Babylon and the qualitatively new world of God is changed into the alternative between sexual purity and impurity signified by the metaphors of bride and temptress, wife and harlot.

If Revelation's political dualism is understood in terms of conventional, dualistic gender-symbolism, it perpetrates sexist prejudice rather than instilling "hunger and thirst" for a just world. By personifying the two alternative "worlds" as female figures and by using the prophetic metaphor of sexual promiscuity for idolatry, Revelation's rhetoric opens the door for a depoliticized reading. Such a depoliticized reading not only genderizes Revelation's ethical dualism but also moralizes it. It is no longer resistance against oppressive political power but individual moral, and especially sexual, behavior that becomes the theo-ethical criterion for faithful Christian practice.

D. Rhetorical Restraints:
Competing Voices

The rhetorical situation of Revelation that evokes the author's visionary response is not simply generated by the urgency of the sociopolitical-religious situation consisting in harassment and denunciation; it is also occasioned by conflicting symbolic universes and rhetorical struggles over values and status. The actual rhetorical situation of Revelation must then be reconstructed as constituted by three competing discourses. The rhetorical response of the author, that of other Christian prophets, and that of his own Jewish community have shaped the rhetorical situation of Revelation.

Revelation's narrative symbolization represents one response among other competing voices, since persuasive argument becomes necessary in a situation where different possibilities for action exist. Revelation's generic tenor indicates that the book's particular sociopolitical context and rhetorical situation could have evoked several Christian theo-ethical responses which might have been in tension and even in conflict with each other. Thus Revelation's point of view and rhetorical intent can only come to the fore if one reconstructs the rhetorical situation that has engendered John's world of vision in such a way that John's rhetorical world of vision is understood not as the *only* response to its particular historical rhetorical situation, but as *one* response among other competing voices.

The commentary section has pointed to the fact that two alternative theological responses, although submerged, have still been inscribed in the text. John represses both responses by vilifying their advocates and by demonizing them. His vituperation seeks to neutralize and eliminate his rivals by casting doubt on their religious legitimacy. He characterizes his own theological response as coming from heaven and God, but he claims that behind the arguments of his opponents stands Satan. Whereas Revelation uses Satan to characterize the imperial power of Rome and its vassals as oppressive and evil, John's vilification of his opponents does not demonize structures and institutions but individuals who probably were well known to the audience. Revelation's rhetoric thus shares in a potentially dangerous feature of early Christian rhetoric that cultivates a highly polemical stance toward outsiders and dissenters and thereby establishes Christian identity over against "the other." Interpreters reinscribe this rhetorical gesture of vituperation, silencing, and repression when they characterize John's opponents as gnostic heretics or unfaithful Jews.

The first response. The first competing discourse articulated by other Christian prophets does not perceive Roman power as oppressive or judge it as evil. Since John polemicizes against Christians, whom he calls with invectives from the Hebrew Bible—Balaamites, followers of Jezebel, or Nicolaitans—it is difficult to separate their genuine teachings from John's biting polemics. They may have argued that the divinity of the emperor is a constitutional fiction for promoting the civil unity of the Roman Empire. For them, participation in Roman civil religion needed to be understood in political terms as part of one's civic duty. If that is the case, they may have argued, why resist paying ceremonial respect to the image of the emperor? Why not work out a compromise with the imperial powers and cults of Asia Minor and Rome? True, the Romans had executed Jesus as a political criminal, but this happened only because of a political misunderstanding of his theological claim to messiahship.

These Christian prophets could have quoted apostolic precedent for their position. They may have asked: Did not the great apostle Paul preach that Christians should not resist civil authorities but rather to give honor to whom honor is due (Rom 13:7), since authorities and rulers have been appointed by God as God's servants? Not to pay taxes or respect to them would entail religious fanaticism, plain foolishness, or dangerous illusion. Leading Christian prophets in the churches of Asia Minor might have argued along these or similar theological lines. They could have represented a majority opinion since most of the later New Testament writings counsel quiet adaptation to and living peacefully in Greco-Roman society and culture.

Interestingly, one of these influential leaders is a woman who could claim the official title "prophet." In contrast, John never applies the title of prophet to himself, probably because his prophetic title was controverted. John, however, does not argue against this woman prophet because she claimed prophetic office and leadership as a woman. Rather he calls her names because he does not agree with her teachings.

This reference to a leading woman indicates not only that women belonged to the target audience of Revelation but also that they were leading figures in the Christian communities of Asia Minor. Such influential leadership of women in the Asian churches is quite in keeping with the general religious and political positions as well as sociocultural influence women had in Asia Minor. An inscription from Smyrna, dating from the second or third century, mentions a Jewish woman by the name of Rufina who was president of the synagogue and the builder of the tomb. This inscription testifies that at least some Jewish women had so much property at their disposal that they could build synagogues, own slaves and set them free, as well as officiate as leaders in the synagogue.

The alternative Christian prophetic group headed by the woman prophet, whose real name is lost to us, appears to have approved of Christian participation in pagan cultic meals and in the imperial cult, a praxis which John consistently labels as "fornication" or "adultery." They may have argued that if well-to-do people benefited from eating sacrificial meat at ceremonial banquets and business occasions, it was even more important that poor people could do so because they rarely could afford to enrich their diet with meat.

The expressions "eating meat sacrificed to idols" and to "know the deep things of Satan" give some clues to their theological argument and its legitimization. Like the Corinthians and Paul, they probably argued that idols are nothing and that an idol has no real power over those whom Christ has redeemed from the cosmic powers of this world. Therefore, participation in the everyday life of Greco-Roman society and in the formalities of the imperial cult would be perfectly harmless for a Spirit-filled Christian. The powers of God and Christ constituted a completely different order from that of Rome's political-religious order (for such an argument, see John 18:36ff).

Like the author of the First Epistle of Peter, who also wrote to Christians in Asia Minor toward the end of the first century, they might have insisted: "Be subject for the Lord's sake to every human institution, whether it be the emperor as supreme or the governors. . . . Fear God. Honor the emperor" (1 Pet 2:13f, 17). Canonical writings such as 1 Peter or the Pastoral Epistles, which encourage quiet adaptation to society, also advocate an ethos of patriarchal submission; however, the text of Revelation gives no indication that the Christian prophets attacked by John have promoted such patriarchalizing tendencies. The opposite seems to be the case, since one of their most eminent leaders is a woman prophet.

It appears that their difference in theological perspective is not primarily doctrinal, since John knows and reveals to the audience the "deep things" of the divine and the demonic. Rather, their disagreement seems rooted in a quite different experience and evaluation of Roman power and influence in Asia Minor. Although we do not know the social status of the prophetic Christian group with whom John competes, we do know that some of the communities to whom he writes have experienced poverty, banishment, violence, and assassination, but others have not. John has only praise for those communities that are poor and have experienced harassment from their Greco-Roman, Asian, and Jewish neighbors. In contrast, he harshly criticizes the community of Laodicea, which considers itself rich and prosperous.

Moreover, it may be significant that the rival woman prophet is likened to the Phoenician princess Jezebel. The choice of the slanderous name of Jezebel might be due not only to the fact that Queen Jezebel supported pagan religious practices and opposed the prophets of Yahweh. It may also allude to the high status and wealth of the woman prophet because Jezebel had the means to back some 850 prophets of Baal and Asherah, and she exercised great influence and power in Israel (1 Kgs 16–21; 2 Kgs 9–10).

The prophetic woman leader in Thyatira is, as far as we know, the first Christian woman who has fallen victim to such vilifying intra-Christian rhetoric. She is historically still visible to us, although her real name is forever lost to historical silence. Because of John's vitriolic rhetoric, this woman prophet has been forever associated in Christian memory not only with heresy and idolatry but also with sexual misconduct. Like the historical queen Jezebel, she has served in Western thought as the archetype of the sexually dangerous woman. During the time of slavery, for instance, the image of Jezebel, the whore, became the controlling image of black womanhood in white, elite, male propaganda.

The second response. The second debate that is repressed but still traceable is the author's argument with segments of the Jewish community in Asia Minor. John mentions twice those who "claim to be Jews, but are not" and calls them the "synagogue of Satan." Archeological and literary sources indicate that the Jewish community in each of the cities mentioned in Revelation was well integrated into both the colonial Roman and the indigenous Asian cultures. They did not live in a Jewish ghetto but had social intercourse with their neighbors and held local municipal, provincial, and imperial offices.

Jewish Sardians, Antiochenes, or Ephesians, for instance, were participating in the gymnasia and in public ceremonies. They held reserved seats in the theater, engaged in all normal occupations, organized in guild and trade associations, spoke the language, and kept the traditions of their cities in which they had lived for centuries—all while still maintaining their own religious and cultural identity. Roman protection and privileges—such as the right to assemble in synagogues for worship and study, to observe Jewish laws and customs, to build synagogues and to receive funds, as well as to be exempt from military service and participation in Roman civil religion—were granted to Jewish communities in Asia throughout the Hellenistic and Roman periods.

The conflict between the Jewish community and some Christian (i.e., messianic) Jews seems to have arisen in social locations where the Christian community was disadvantaged. The message to Smyrna (2:8-11) speaks of the community's tribulation and poverty in connection with the slander of "those who say that they are Jews but are not. . . ." John praises the community of Philadelphia (3:7-13) for having kept Christ's word and for not having denied the name of the One who has the key of David. Smyrna and Philadelphia are said to have "little power" and to experience slander, poverty, tribulation, imprisonment, and threat to life. They are the only communities that receive solely praise and no censure.

It is difficult to say whether those who "claim to be Jews but are not" are Jews in general or Jews who are Christians. The latter is possible, because at the time of Revelation, Christians like John were still members of the Jewish community and represented a particular party or group within Judaism similar to that of the Pharisees or the Essenes. In any case, John's high appreciation for Judaism expresses itself not only in his choice of traditional Jewish language and symbolism but also in that he denies his rivals the title of honor, "Jew," and instead calls them "synagogue of Satan."

Why would Jews slander other "Christian" Jews and cause difficulties and persecution for them? The promise of eschatological reversal in 3:9 indicates that the conflict was one of honor and legitimacy. If John responds in kind, then their slander consists probably in the fact that in Smyrna and Philadelphia they withheld the prerogatives and legitimacy of Judaism from the local Christian-Jewish assembly. They may have done so in order to distance themselves from those who were poor and had little power but much messianic fervor.

If this is the case, then the conflict between Jewish coreligionists in Smyrna and Philadelphia was of a religious-political nature. Those Jews who had become well-respected members of their Asian communities and were enjoying the privileges granted by Rome to the Jewish community probably felt the political need to distance themselves from messianic revolutionary groups. They had good reasons for doing so, because not only in Palestine but also in the Greco-Roman dispersion such groups were said to incite rebellion against Rome. Some such conflict in values and status over "true Judaism" could become a matter of survival for those Christians identified as Jewish messianists.

John's interpretation of the actual sociopolitical rhetorical situation deepens this rhetorical-political conflict by linking the difficulties among Jews and Christians of different persuasions with eschatological tribulations, imprisonment, and death. It seems to be John who encodes this rhetorical struggle over status, identity, and values as a site of conflicts over "genuine Jewish" policy and religious-political strategy toward the imperial power and civil religion of Rome. He does so in a historical situation where Jewish Christians are a religious minority group without rights and power.

After the separation of Judaism and Christianity into two different religions and the political ascendancy of Christianity after the demise of the Roman Empire, the rhetorical situation of those reading Revelation has drastically changed. Christian preachers who today repeat John's charge against Judaism as "being the synagogue of Satan" do so in a hegemonic rhetorical situation, where Jews belong to an often maligned minority group. Revelation's defensive rhetoric of self-preservation of Jewish identity has been turned into a language of hate. Throughout the centuries and still today, John's vilification of his coreligionists has evoked the Christian response of anti-Judaism, engendering the vilification and persecution of true Judaism. Such vilification is often still legitimated by Revelation's claim to be the reliable "word of God."

The response of John. In such a situation of competing prophetic voices and theological perspectives, it becomes necessary for John to establish the trustworthiness and "truth" of his rhetorical world of vision. The assertion of Revelation's authority and trustworthiness (ethos) is repeated throughout the book but is especially found at its beginning and end. Contrary to apocalyptic convention John acknowledges his own authorship and situates himself as contemporary with his audience in order to establish his ethos, or credibility.

Although Revelation calls itself the revelation of Jesus Christ, it is generally known as the "Revelation of John." This title was added only when the book was accepted into the canon. Tradition, therefore, has ascribed Revelation to the apostle John, even though the author does not claim such a title for himself but refers to the twelve apostles as great figures of the past (21:14). Today, most scholars believe that the book is not pseudonymous but authored by a Jewish Christian seer named John.

Unlike other apocalyptic writers, John does not intend to establish the ethos of his discourse by projecting the speaker back in time in order to tell past history in the form of future prediction. Revelation's images and visions may therefore not be interpreted as retrojected historical description or projected future prediction of end-timetables or actual events in salvation history. The author does not have much more information about the end time than do the authors of the Synoptic apocalypse (Mark 13 and its parallels) or 1 Thess 4:13ff; 1 Cor 15:20ff; or 2 Thess 2:1ff. Revelation's dramatic presentation only expands upon these early Christian expectations with the help of traditional language and contemporary images.

Clearly John does not seek to establish his ethos in terms of apostolic authority but in terms of prophetic authority. He does so not by claiming prophetic authorship and status for himself but by declaring God and Christ as the authors of his prophetic-apocalyptic letter. He insists that the trustworthiness of his visionary narrative does not depend on his own authority but relies on that of God and Christ. Again, such a practice of appealing to external authorities as guarantors for a given position is pervasive in early Christian literature in contradistinction to classical rhetoric, where argument is grounded in cultural convention. It has had dangerous consequences in the history of Christianity because in its doctrinal and institutionalized form it has silenced all critique of ecclesiastical and civil authority.

The introduction to Revelation establishes a chain of revelatory authority which resides with God and is communicated through Christ or the angelic interpreter to John and through him to the audience. Strictly speaking the "words of prophecy" do not represent John's discourse but rather claim to be divine discourse. The *real* authors of Revelation are God, the risen Jesus, and the sevenfold Spirit. John does present himself not as author but as their mouthpiece and scribe. The One in Human Likeness and the Spirit "speak" to the churches, and John merely transcribes their message (1:11, 19; 2:1—3:22).

In addition, John does not only bless those who read, hear, and keep the words of prophecy (Rev 1:3; 22:7) but also adds a curse at the end (22:18-19). Although it was not usual for ancient writers to attempt to secure a faithful transmission of their work, he threatens anyone who would add something with the plagues which the book describes. Analogously, he warns against subtracting anything from the content of the book. Such a powerful adjuration indicates that John is not sure how his work will be received and respected. John seems to want to forestall the discussion and testing of his work. His sanction against anyone who would alter the text contradicts his repeated hermeneutical statements that invite the audience to participate actively in the process of interpretation.

It was a commonplace assumption in early Christianity that prophecy required the discernment of the Spirit and the testing of the prophets. John's vilification of his prophetic rivals and his repeated rhetorical stress on Revelation's heavenly ratification and divine sanction evidence a great anxiety about the authority and influence of his work. They characterize John's discourse as belonging to that of a cognitive minority within the Christian community of Asia.

John's insistence on the divine authorship of Revelation has decisively influenced Christian understanding of canonical authority and revelation. If one accepts his portrayal of the revelatory process, one comes to an understanding of Scripture as the dictated "word of God" rather than as the rhetorical response of the biblical writer to a particular theo-ethical problem and socio-rhetorical location. Biblical readers often neglect the early Christian insight that the Spirit must be *discerned* and the words and life-style of prophets must be *tested* by the community. What the Spirit says today to our own particular sociopolitical location and rhetorical situation must be assessed in a theo-ethical practice of rhetorical interpretation that can trace God's power for justice and salvation in our own political and personal struggles for liberation.

In conclusion, the rhetorical reconstruction of Revelation's sociohistorical location and its contextualization in present-day interpretation have important implications for a hermeneutic of proclamation. The understanding and evaluation of Revelation and its theo-ethical world of vision depend very much on how exegetes reconstruct its rhetorical-historical place. Revelation's rhetorical practice can be comprehended only in interaction with its historical and rhetorical contexts.

Moreover, Revelation's message must be understood as directed to a particular historical-rhetorical condition and can not simply be "translated," or applied, to any situation. Only where a rhetorical situation similar to that addressed by Revelation exists can Revelation's world of vision be understood as a "fitting" theo-ethical response. Wherever such a situation does not persist, the rhetorical power of John's vision does not engender resistance but rather evokes resentment or projects evil onto others. Wherever a totally different rhetorical situation exists, the book no longer elicits a fitting response.

Such an understanding of Revelation as a particular rhetorical-theological practice does not mean that one has to accept its world of vision without reservation and critique. It also does not necessitate that Revelation's rhetoric appeals only to readers who experience injustice and oppression. Without question, this biblical book has been and is attractive to all kinds of people in very different sociopolitical situations and walks of life. It is utilized by those in power for making doomsday predictions and for justifying wars, as well as by those projecting their hatreds and fears on others.

The only point I want to make here is that Revelation will elicit a fitting theo-ethical response only in those sociopolitical situations that cry out for justice. When Christian groups are excluded from political power, Revelation's language of divine kingship and royal reward, as well as its ethical dualism, stands against unjust authority and champions the oppressed and disenfranchised. Whenever Christians join the power structures of their society and seek to stabilize them, the same rhetorical world of vision serves to sacralize dominant authorities and preach revenge against their enemies.

My point is simple. I am arguing here that we should not reduce the reader of Revelation to a timeless, ideal reader, because by so doing, we essentialize and dehistoricize the book and our own readings. Rather than pose an abstract-reader and universalized-rhetorical situation, we must not only detect and articulate our own presuppositions, interests, emotions, and sociopolitical locations in an explicit way, but we must sort out what kind and quality of theo-ethical response becomes dominant in our own readings. Reading and preaching Revelation does not mean to repeat the book's "first" meanings but to engage both critically and responsibly its rhetorical world of vision in our own struggles for justice and liberation.

SELECTED BIBLIOGRAPHY

The format of the Proclamation Commentaries series precludes extensive footnotes. I regret that I am therefore not able officially to acknowledge my debt to the many scholars with whom I am in conversation and from whom I have learned much about the book of Revelation and its sociohistorical location. I do hope that this commentary will make a contribution to this ongoing conversation on Revelation.

This selected bibliography mentions only recent works, all but one in English, that have appeared in the past decade and have been primary dialogue-partners in revising this book. It is divided into general works on interpretation, collections of essays that reflect the present status of scholarship, and commentaries/monographs with alternative interpretations and extensive bibliographical information.

Interpretation

Cameron, Deborah. *Feminism and Linguistic Theory*. London: Macmillan & Co., 1985.

Croatto, J. Severin. *Biblical Hermeneutics*. Maryknoll, N.Y.: Orbis Books, 1987.

Harlow, Barbara. *Resistance Literature*. New York: Methuen, 1987.

Mack, Burton L. *Rhetoric and the New Testament*. Minneapolis: Fortress Press, 1990.

Mosala, Itumeleng J. *Biblical Hermeneutics and Black Theology in South Africa*. Grand Rapids: Wm. B. Eerdmans Publishing Co., 1989.

Rowland, C., and M. Carver. *Liberating Exegesis: The Challenge of Liberation Theology for Biblical Studies*. London: SPCK, 1990.

Schüssler Fiorenza, Elisabeth. *Bread Not Stone: The Challenge of Feminist Biblical Interpretation*. Boston: Beacon Press, 1984.

Wuellner, Wilhelm. "Hermeneutics and Rhetorics. From 'Truth and Method' to 'Truth and Power,'" *Scriptura S* 3 (1989) 1–54.

Collections of Essays

Hellholm, David, ed. *Apocalypticism in the Mediterranean World and the Near East. Proceedings of the International Colloquium on Apocalypticism, Uppsala, 1979*. Tübingen: J. C. B. Mohr, 1983.

Interpretation, 40, no. 3 (July 1986).

Lambrecht, Jan. *L' Apopcalypse johannique et l'Apocalyptique dans le Nouveau Testament*. Louvain: University Press, 1980.

Yarbro Collins, Adela, ed. "Early Christian Apocalypticism: Genre and Social Setting." *Semeia* 36 (1986).

Loeb Classical Library. 475 vols. Cambridge: Harvard University Press, 1920–91.

Commentaries/Monographs

Aune, David E. *Prophecy in Early Christianity and the Ancient Mediterranean World*. Grand Rapids: Wm. B. Eerdmans Publishing Co., 1983.

———. "Revelation." In *Harpers Bible Commentary*, edited by James L. Mays, et al., 1300–19. San Francisco: Harper & Row, 1988.

Berrigan, Daniel. *The Nightmare of God*. Portland, Oreg.: Sunburst Press, 1983.

Boesak, Allan A. *Comfort and Protest: The Apocalypse from a South African Perspective*. Philadelphia: The Westminster Press, 1987.

Boring, M. Eugene. *Revelation: Interpretation*. Louisville: John Knox Press, 1989.

Collins, John J. *The Apocalyptic Imagination*. New York: Crossroad/Continuum Publishing Group, 1987.

Court, John. M. *Myth and History in the Book of Revelation*. Atlanta: John Knox Press, 1979.

Halsell, Grace. *Prophecy and Politics. Militant Evangelists on the Road to Nuclear War*. Westport, Conn.: Lawrence Hill & Co., 1986.

Hemer, Colin J. *The Letters to the Seven Churches of Asia in Their Local Setting*. Sheffield: JSOT Press, 1986.

Jeske, Richard L. *Revelation for Today: Images of Hope*. Philadelphia: Fortress Press, 1983.

Kealy, S. P. *The Apopcalypse of John*. Wilmington, Del.: Glazier, 1987.

Krodel, Gerhard A. *Revelation*. Augsburg Commentary on the New Testament. Minneapolis: Augsburg, 1989.

Lindsey, Hal. *The Late Great Planet Earth*. Grand Rapids: Zondervan Publishing House, 1970.

Pippin, Tina. "Political Reality and the Liberating Vision: The Context of the Book of Revelation." Diss., Southern Baptist Theological Seminary, Louisville, 1987.

Price, S. R. F. *Rituals and Power: The Roman Imperial Cult in Asia Minor*. Cambridge: Cambridge University Press, 1984.

Ruiz, Jean-Pierre. *Ezekiel in the Apocalypse: The Transformation of Prophetic Language in Revelation 16:17—19:10*. Frankfurt: Peter Lang, 1989.

Schüssler Fiorenza, Elisabeth. *The Book of Revelation: Justice and Judgement*. Philadelphia: Fortress Press, 1985.

————, "Revelation." In *The Books of the Bible*, edited by B. W. Anderson, vol. 2, 367–81. New York: Charles Scribner's Sons, 1989.

Thompson, Leonard L. *The Book of Revelation: Apocalypse and Empire.* Oxford: Oxford University Press, 1990.

Walvoord, John F. *Armageddon, Oil and the Middle East Crisis.* 2d ed. Grand Rapids: Zondervan Publishing House, 1990.

Yamauchi, Edwin. *The Archaeology of New Testament Cities in Western Asia Minor.* Grand Rapids: Baker Book House, 1980.

Yarbro Collins, Adela. *Crisis and Catharsis: The Power of the Apocalypse.* Philadelphia: The Westminster Press, 1984.

————. "The Apocalypse (Revelation)." In *The New Jerome Biblical Commentary*, edited by Raymond E. Brown, et al., 996–1016. Englewood Cliffs, N.J.: Prentice-Hall, 1990.

INDEX